THE
LAST CAMPAIGN

Grant Saves the Union

GREAT BATTLES OF HISTORY

Hanson W. Baldwin, *General Editor*

THE LAST CAMPAIGN

Grant Saves the Union

by
Earl Schenck Miers

Illustrated with Maps

J. B. Lippincott Company
Philadelphia & New York

Contents

MAPS

I

Dramatis Personae

The final act of national tragedy approached. The four leading actors—Jefferson Davis and Abraham Lincoln, Robert E. Lee and Ulysses S. Grant—were cast in roles they were incapable of changing. Each now played a part he never had wanted and each, as a result, suffered scars upon mind and heart. Each prayed to the same God that the conflict soon would end. Each shed silent tears for his dead, his maimed, his imprisoned, his homeless. Each was trapped by the overwhelming momentum of a civil war that found conflicting cultures within the same society struggling for a political power all four called liberty. Each had only his own dignity and self-respect for which to struggle, for the end of the war became inevitable when through the Emancipation Proclamation the North added a moral purpose that the South could not match. Thus the hope for foreign intervention, without which the South could not win, was blasted by the response of the working classes in England and France to a document which the majority did not fully understand. But the triumph for the North was devastating nonetheless. The War Between the States could never become a Vietnam.

More than the others, Jefferson Davis was baffled and frustrated by the unfolding climax. He could not accept its reality. His wife Varina remembered the Confederate President who had been the life of a party and had romped joyously with children. But then came 1863 and Gettysburg. Jefferson Davis never sang again. Toward dusk, in the last winter of the war, he would mount his fine Arabian horse and ride alone through the streets of Richmond. To Varina the effect was far more ghastly than the stench that sometimes rose from the James River. In these moments she cowered in a chair, as though a knife were pointed at her heart, for there were so many who might attack her husband—Negroes, Union prisoners escaped from the city jail, vindictive members of the Confederate Congress who wished the war finished.[1] Davis rode on oblivious to those around him, so steeped was he in his own problems, sorrows, and memories.

The Confederate President's recollections rarely, if ever, rose above the bittersweet. His happiest moments of the war came in February, 1861, waiting at his plantation in Mississippi in anticipation of his appointment as field commander of the army. But for all that Montgomery, Alabama, had exhausted itself by turning over its beautiful capitol to the delegates of the Provisional Confederate Congress and had loaned those gentlemen $500,000 to finance their activities, the Montgomery story developed numerous unpleasant surprises. Forty-six delegates, divided almost equally between Whigs and Democrats, represented the first six seceding states.[2] If familiar faces appeared in the lobbies of the Exchange Hotel and Montgomery House, that fact was small wonder: the majority had served in the United States Congress. Georgia and South Carolina dominated the convention, for fourteen of their eighteen delegates had learned the art of government in Washington.

Georgia brought three prospective candidates for the presidency: Howell Cobb (former United States Secretary of the Treasury), Robert Toombs, and Alexander H. Stephens. South Carolina settled on two: Robert Barnwell Rhett and William L. Yancey. Tensions emerged. Rhett and Yancey were too outspoken fire-eaters to satisfy either the more northern or as yet uncommitted border states. Stephens was an avowed anti-secessionist. In the universal belief that the Confederacy could never succeed without the support of Virginia, an Alabaman with intimate knowledge of the Old Dominion State spoke passionately of why Virginia would accept no one but a conservative in the presidency. Yancey withdrew. Obviously a compromise was needed, and so on the first ballot Jefferson Davis was unanimously chosen. Psychologically, Davis was as much a "minority" President in the South as Lincoln was in the North. Nor would Lincoln ever hate any member of his official family more bitterly or longer than Davis despised that ultra-conservative, Vice-President Stephens.[3]

Next a permanent Confederate government was adopted, not altogether to Davis's joy. The final Confederate Constitution varied from the Federal by ensuring the supremacy of the states, sanctifying slavery but forbidding the slave trade, and limiting the President to one six-year term. There were to be no subsidies, no protective tariffs, no contractor's jobs, no financial manipulation, no legislation or taxation for the "general welfare." [4] Davis's poker face looked like the frozen "phiz" on the Confederate postage stamp when, following the governmental structure in Washington, he was forced to work through the chairman of congressional committees of legislation, finance, foreign affairs, military affairs, and naval affairs. Stephens was chairman of one committee, and disappointed contenders for the presidency chaired two others.

Davis's mind worked sincerely, if methodically, with the legislative processes of the Confederacy, but his heart never left the battlefield. He was, after all, a graduate of West Point, Class of 1828; he had served seven years on the Northwest frontier; he had fought in the Mexican War and been severely wounded at Buena Vista; and he had been Franklin Pierce's Secretary of War, where his only ineptness had been trying to patrol American deserts by camelback. Lee was the one general he held in awe; and although Davis's autobiography abounds with banal clichés concerning the charm, bravery, chivalry, wisdom, and wit of his generals, he was simply revealing anew that memoirs and official records are written to conceal as well as to reveal the truth.

With grandfatherly indulgence, Jefferson Davis advised Confederate troops, "Never be haughty to the humble, or humble to the haughty." The statement was remarkable only to the extent that, to the bottom of his heels, Davis was a social snob. After three years of war no one was any longer a stranger. The Confederate President could not disguise his obstinacy, his quickness to take umbrage at personal criticism, his contempt for public opinion, his poor judgment of faults and virtues within his "pets," his eternal fussing over small details. To South Carolina's influential Senator James Henry Hammond he was "as vain as a peacock, as ambitious as the Devil." With reluctance Robert G. H. Kean, Chief of the Bureau of War, confessed to his diary as early as November, 1862, "I am coming to Mr. [Frank G.] Ruffin's opinion. He says he used to think Jefferson Davis a *mule*, but a *good mule*. He has come to think him a jackass." That once presidential hopeful, Rhett, who was also editor of the Charleston *Mercury* and who often seemed educated above his own intelligence, characterized Davis as "not only a dishonest honest man but also a liar." [5]

In the last winter of war, 1864–65, as Jefferson Davis walked south from his domestic quarters in the Brockenborough Mansion to his offices in the magnificent Capitol that Thomas Jefferson had designed in Richmond, the President's heart knew what his mind would not admit: the war was winding down. Inflation, running rampant over the South, led to food riots and broke fighting morale. Davis knew of the Whigs who had taken to calling him a tyrant; of the conspiracy of "original secessionists" and "eleventh-hour men," led by Governors Brown of Georgia and Vance of North Carolina, who plotted to depose him; of the congressmen who, with the Negro freed and thus counting a full vote instead of the three-fifths vote of antebellum days, wished to return to Washington so that they could gain as quickly as possible power over the influential congressional committees.[6]

The facial neuralgia which long had afflicted Davis was running its full course. The President's nerves were shattered, his health failing, and in all probability, considering the indignities that still faced him, he never recovered completely. Rumored proposals that the Cabinet had decided to make Lee dictator amused him because he knew that Lee possessed less interest and knowledge of politics than the head of a pin. Aside from the fact that the Union President also claimed Kentucky as a birthplace, Davis never accepted Lincoln as an equal; he belonged to that school of scriveners and historians who, perversely and inexplicably, thought the South was greater if it lost to pygmies rather than to giants. Nowhere in the two volumes of Jefferson Davis's *Rise and Fall of the Confederate Government* is there a clear, compassionate, comprehensible image of the true Lincoln; least of all in those last fatal hours could Davis recognize that his failure rested not within his stars but within himself and the man of epic vision who occupied the White House.

On a day in July, 1847, that celebrated Illinois Congressman, Elihu B. Washburne of Galena, was talking to a group of friends beneath the balcony of Chicago's Sherman House. In the group was Lisle Smith—"accomplished scholar and unrivaled orator"— who, glancing up suddenly, exclaimed, "There is Lincoln on the other side of the street. Just look at 'Old Abe.' "

The nickname stuck, seeming to belong, as the man who bore it, to the age and world that produced Tom Sawyer and Huckleberry Finn. Lincoln's appearance that day Washburne found unforgettable: "Tall, angular and awkward, he had on a short-waisted, thin swallow-tail coat, a short vest of the same material, thin pantaloons, scarcely coming to his ankles, a straw hat and a pair of brogans with woolen socks." Laughter surrounded Old Abe. In 1848, when Lincoln campaigned for Zachary Taylor over Martin Van Buren, the *Democratic Free Press* of Peoria described the political style of the man from Springfield: "Mr. Lincoln blew his nose, bobbed his head, threw up his coat tail, and in the course of two hours was delivered of a vast amount of 'sound and fury.'" Lincoln accepted such banter good-humoredly, and the *Central Transcript* of Clinton commented that "he greets everybody, and everybody greets him . . . the poorest and plainest amongst our people, fears not to approach, and never fails to receive a hearty welcome from him."

Lad of the Kentucky hills and Indiana forests, gangling farm-hand, rail-splitter and shopkeeper, self-taught surveyor and lawyer, hesitant suitor, indulgent husband and father, statesman schooled in the rough-and-tumble of prairie politics—nowhere in Lincoln's career was there the tiniest hint that one day he would become the sixteenth President of the United States. He lived with ideas, turning them over and polishing them in his mind until they acquired a gemlike quality. Thus he asked a friend, "Can we, as a nation, continue together *permanently—forever*—half slave, half free?" Less than three years later this question had blossomed into the "House-Divided Speech" that brought him to national attention and ultimately carried him to Washington. Friends told him in advance that it was "a damned fool utterance," but upon occasion, when he felt supremely self-confident, Lincoln would not budge.

Billy Herndon, Lincoln's law partner, was often outraged by Old Abe's essential character. Billy liked hard liquor, as much as he could get of it, whereas Lincoln was a temperance man, yet (perhaps to spare Billy's sensitivities) he was never a rabid cold-water crusader. Billy was a stanch abolitionist; Lincoln would ride ten miles rather than be caught at an abolition meeting. Billy was an atheist and was outraged when told Lincoln had called the New Testament "the rock on which I stand." Herndon knew otherwise; he knew the Lincoln who dripped with melancholy, and that fellow, by God, was an infidel! Again, possibly to mollify Billy, Lincoln noted the announcement at the Christian Church on the "Second Coming of Christ" and quipped, "It is my considered opinion that, if the Lord has been in Springfield once, he will never come the second time." But there were many sides to Lincoln that Billy never gleaned. In reviewing the close of the national tragedy, Lord Charnwood, among the first good Lincoln biographers, characterized Lincoln's Second Inaugural as a masterpiece of "religious feelings," and he judged why Lincoln had scaled intellectual Olympian heights: "This man had stood alone in the dark. He had done justice; he had loved mercy; he had walked humbly with God."

When Lincoln left for Washington, an astute Herndon wrote Senator Henry Wilson of Massachusetts, "You and I must keep the people right; God will keep Lincoln right." He could be, as Carl Sandburg wrote, "hard as rock and soft as drifting fog.". Secretary of State William H. Seward, who believed he should have been President and took Lincoln for a country bumpkin to be managed as a figurehead while Seward wielded the power, quickly was taught his lesson. Seward's plan of reuniting North and South in common cause by picking a war with England, Spain, or France—or all three, if necessary—was rejected out of hand; and when the South feared, as Lincoln believed, that secessions tend to wither in the sunlight, Seward was among the connivers who provoked an unnecessary war at Fort Sumter. Lincoln resisted by using the same militia power George Washington had invoked in crushing the Whiskey Rebellion.[7] Jefferson Davis never forgave the crushing logic with which Lincoln justified his action to a special session of Congress:

It might seem, at first thought, to be of little difference whether the present movement at the South be called "secession" or "rebellion." The movers, however, well understand the difference. At the beginning, they knew they could never raise their treason to any respectable magnitude, by any name which implies *violation* of law. They knew their people possessed as much of moral sense, as much of devotion to law and order, and as much pride in, and reverence for, the history, and government, of their common country, as any other civilized, and patriotic people. They knew they could make no advancement directly in the teeth of these strong and noble sentiments. Accordingly they commenced by an insidious debauching of the public mind. They invented an ingenious sophism, which, if conceded, was followed by perfectly logical steps, through all the incidents, to the complete destruction of the Union. The sophism itself is, that any state of the Union may, *consistently* with the national Constitution, and therefore *lawfully*, and *peacefully*, withdraw from the Union, without the consent of the Union, or of any other state. The little disguise that the supposed right is to be exercised only for just cause, themselves to be the sole judge of its justice, is too thin to merit any notice.[8]

Very few men who lived in the White House ever possessed less personal military experience than Lincoln. As a captain in the Black Hawk War—so elected by his own company of youthful volunteers in New Salem—he made a great many charges on mosquitoes and wild onion patches but never sighted a live Indian. As a congressman for two years he was a consistent and vociferous dove toward the Mexican War, which he considered immoral and illegal.

Lincoln was, as Charles A. Dana realized, "all solid, hard, keen intelligence combined with goodness." The miracle of the result was how, when the war ended on the battlefield, the true victory belonged to the heart of humanity. Looking at the problems afresh, as they developed in this last act of the tragedy, one understands why this first war to be fought with the tools and weapons of the Industrial Revolution severely tested the mental capacities of its chief participants.[9] What now the American-at-war was forced to teach himself began as the range of his killing power expanded. Sensibly the fields over which he fought became honeycombed with defense lines; thereafter flexible formations and swift outflanking movements offered practically the only chance of success in battle.

Blurred though the martial picture is, it constitutes the first glimpse anyone would have of what today we call total war. In the grand art of killing one's fellow men, this more sophisticated form, with its attendant perplexities of transportation, supply, and finance, may have staggered American imaginations, but there is nothing in the record to show that European observers on the scene were learning as much or as well. Lincoln, an avid student of Shakespeare, realized that no tragedy was complete without its redeeming catharsis, a theme underscored by his Gettysburg Address and Second Inaugural; no one comprehended more deeply than he that when all the bills were paid for moving all the men and weapons to all the fields of battle, the victory of arms amounted to little unless a victory of the human spirit also was won.

Once, in the final phase of the conflict Lincoln gazed into a mirror and saw himself as a double image. The President shivered slightly, recalling the frontier superstition that this kind of phenomenon presaged the approach of death.

As the threat of secession advanced—this menace, in the opinion of Robert E. Lee, that would leave the country between "a state of anarchy and civil war"—it was natural for Lee to read Nicholl Everett's *Life of Washington*.[10] Few must be the cases where father and son became leading figures in America's two civil wars—the Revolution and the Rebellion,[11] both fought within less than a century.

Well could Robert be proud of the military record of his sire, Major General Henry "Light-Horse Harry" Lee, who was only twenty-one when he entered the Revolution and won his first fame as the "boy commander." After Valley Forge and the skirmish at Spread Eagle Inn (1781), Congress commended him for the "distinguished honor" with which he behaved. His creation of Lee's Legion and its brilliant fighting in other theaters of the war brought him further laurels, and he received one of the eight medals voted in gratitude by Congress during the course of the Revolution.

Unfortunately for Robert, the impulses and optimism that had carried Light-Horse Harry to glory in war failed him in peace. Bad judgment in land speculations led to his imprisonment, and in jail he foolishly expected to recoup his fortune by writing his memoirs. His ill luck continued after his iron gate swung open. His opposition to the War of 1812 developed his friendship with Alexander C. Hanson, editor of the *Baltimore Federal Republican*, whose antiwar editorials so inflamed Baltimore mobs that they wrecked his plant, press and building. A stubborn Hanson refused to cease publication, having the paper printed in Georgetown while he continued living in Baltimore. The old soldier in Light-Horse Harry could not resist helping Hanson. Being present in the structure that Hanson combined into office and residence when another wrathful mob attacked, he barricaded the house, distributed guns to Hanson and the few friends with him, and placed the little garrison into strategic positions. Gunshots rang out, killing one member of the mob and wounding another. The militia arrived to break up the assault, but next morning the mob returned and so, too, did the militia. Light-Horse Harry agreed that his garrison would be safer in jail. Afterward a howling, drunken mob broke open the door and overpowered the jailer. The elder Lee was dreadfully treated. Penknives repeatedly stabbed his body and candle grease was poured into his eyes; one brute attempted to cut off his nose.[12] Light-Horse Harry tried to heal his shattered health in the Caribbean but weakened steadily; he died during the journey home and was buried at Cumberland Island, Georgia.

These events defined the limits of R. E. Lee's career. He gave up the play of other boys to hurry home from school and take his invalid mother for a drive in the carriage or to afternoon tea with her friends, which explains why he was always more comfortable in the company of women. When his mother complained of colds or drafts, he cut squares of newspaper to cover the windows of the old family coach. "If Robert left the room," a relative said, "she kept her eyes on the door till he returned." Appointed to West Point while John C. Calhoun was Secretary of War, Robert graduated second in his class and received no demerits. In 1830 he married the daughter of

George Washington's adopted son. Lee served as an army engineer, fought through the Mexican War (bringing home, unopened, the bottle of brandy he had taken for possible "medicinal" use), and became for a time superintendent of West Point. His horizons, physical and spiritual, were based on the quiet lawyer culture of Old Virginia. Wherever crossroads offered a central meeting place between towns, there rose a little courthouse, a tavern, a store, a few houses, and an orderly system of life based on reason, justice, and experience. Orange Court House, Culpeper Court House, Spotsylvania Court House—how well Robert knew and loved these sleepy villages; in the mountains between Richmond and Lynchburg was another named Appomattox Court House.

The mere suggestion of secession enraged Lee. Slavery, he told his wife, was "a greater evil to the white man than to the black." He wrote a Northern cousin, Markie Williams, "I only see that a fearful calamity is upon us, and fear that the country will have to pass through for its sins a fiery ordeal." At that moment he was more perceptive than Lincoln in sensing the onrushing tragedy. When the blandishments of the agents from Montgomery overcame the violent opposition of Governor Sam Houston and Texas joined the Confederacy, Lee, then stationed in Texas, resigned from the army and returned to Virginia. He expressed his frustration to his eldest son, Custis; those " 'Cotton States,' as they term themselves," he said, were eager for "the renewal of the slave trade," a plan to which he was opposed "on every ground."

The torment that Virginia might secede, his wife declared, cost him "tears of blood." He was offered a brigadier generalship by the Confederate army but did not reply to the letter; a commission as colonel in the U. S. cavalry, signed by Lincoln, Lee accepted. But then Virginia left the Union. "I am one of those dull creatures that cannot see the good of secession," he said bitterly on hearing the news. At home that night he paced yard and bedroom and toward midnight knelt in prayer, making his peace with God. He could no more forsake a troubled Virginia than an invalid mother.

Since love motivated Lee, he fought desperately and brilliantly. Outwardly his calm became an inspiration throughout the South, yet inwardly burned a spark of the impulsive emotionalism that had doomed Light-Horse Harry. At Fredericksburg he remarked that it was well war was awful or else they all would begin to enjoy it too much. General James B. Longstreet described him at Gettysburg: "He seemed under a subdued excitement, which occasionally took possession of him when 'the hunt was up,' and threatened his superb equipoise."

The years of war had taken a toll. In 1864–65, as the last campaign approached, Lee's brown hair and beard were turning gray, and in a gray coat mounted on a gray horse, riding into Richmond, he appeared to blend with the dull bituminous smoke of a lowering winter day. He slept in a tent, sharing the hazards and discomforts of his men; he declared that he avoided using Southern mansions for his headquarters so that the Yankees would have no excuse for burning these structures—forgivable propaganda in times of war. Standing straight, his face resolute, his eyes gentle, he became the final symbol of Southern chivalry in arms. To the poet Sidney Lanier, watching Lee sleep through outdoor church services, "As he slumbered . . . it seemed to me as if the present earth floated off through the sunlight and the antique earth returned out of the past and some majestic god sat on a hill sculptured in stone presiding over a terrible yet sublime contest of human passions."

The place was a tavern in Galena, Illinois, and a smart-alecky lawyer, whose favorite avocation was ribbing newcomers, turned on Grant.

"Stranger here?"

"Yes," Grant answered.

"Travel far?"

"Far enough."

"Looks as though you might have traveled through hell."

"I have."

"Well, how did you find things down there?"

"Oh, much the same as in Galena—lawyers nearest the fire."

Historians, both North and South, have been so busy painting a caricature of Grant that it is difficult to recreate the real person. A West Point cadet who fought capably in the Mexican War, Grant was one of those go-ahead Westerners that Anthony Trollope described: "They rarely amuse themselves. Food, newspapers, and brandy-smashes suffice for life; and while these last, whatever may occur, the man is still there in his manhood."

The rumormongers said that Grant was washed out of the army in California for drunkenness, but the Captain told another story. "My family, all this while [1852–54], was at the East. . . . I saw no chance of supporting them on the Pacific coast out of my pay as an army officer."

Grant admitted that he failed as a farmer in Missouri and eked out a slim livelihood for his wife and family by delivering cordwood by the wagonload to St. Louis. Old army friends seeing him there cried, "Good God, Grant, what are you doing?" Grant replied good-humoredly, "I am solving the problem of poverty." He told no one that this was the Christmas (1858) when he pawned his watch to buy presents for his wife and youngsters.

Grant always had detested his father's tannery, but his last recourse was to journey to Galena and take over the family's business. Far from ruining it, he achieved a solid success—so much so that he and his two brothers each drew $600 a year and placed the remaining profits in a trust fund for their three sisters.

In civilian life Grant was a notoriously kind and gentle man. He walked out of a bullfight in Mexico City because he was sickened by the suffering of the animals. On rainy days he romped with his children, sailing paper boats down the gutters of the hill which their brick house topped. Almost as politically naïve as Lee, Grant explained how he had used his franchise in 1856: "I voted for Buchanan because I didn't know him and I voted against Frémont because I did know him." [13]

The war would have passed by Grant had not Galena's Elihu B. Washburne demanded that a place be found for this quiet, thoughtful, undramatic little townsman. Even so, Grant might have smothered in the mudhole of Cairo, Illinois, dreaming how fine it would be to command a cavalry brigade in the Army of the Potomac, had he not forced his own opportunities. After Vicksburg (that terraced city that so largely resembled the approach to Galena), Grant grew in fame.[14]

Those who accuse Grant of ruthlessness add to the caricature by subtracting from the real personality. The wantonness of war touched both sides. The Union's burning of Columbia, South Carolina, was no more reprehensible than the Confederacy's deliberate destruction of Chambersburg, Pennsylvania. Although the evidence is contradictory, *something* happened at Fort Pillow to suggest the horror of Mylai in Vietnam. General Nathan Bedford Forrest's official report admitted "The river was dyed with the blood of the slaughtered troops for 200 yards." William J. Mays, who fought with the 13th Tennessee Cavalry, probably stretched the truth in describing an inflamed Confederate soldier firing on Negro soldiers, women, and children as he cried, "Yes, God damn you, you thought you are free, did you?" And yet Forrest's biographer, John A. Wyeth, confessed, "Human life was held exceeding cheap in 1864, and especially in west Tennessee." [15] As the war wound down, there was ridiculous malice in a Confederate plot to send a band of trained arsonists to burn New York City.

Although Grant's losses were excessive when "hammering" an opponent, earning him the mocking epithet of "butcher," his own soldiers said, "Who's shedding this blood, anyhow? They better wait until we fellows down at the front hollo, 'Enough!'" His powers of concentration were enormous. His field orders were so clear, so concise, so thoroughly thought through that invariably they had to be read only once.[16]

Grant rarely if ever failed to face a duty. An army under then Colonel Albert Sidney Johnston had been sent to Utah to coerce the Mormons into conforming to "public morality" when Lincoln became President, but Old Abe had no notion of dealing with "the twin relics of barbarism, slavery and polygamy." The Morrill Antibigamy Act of 1862, forbidding "celestial marriage" in the territories, was as far as the Lincoln Administration ever moved against the Mormons. Andrew Johnson, Lincoln's successor, had his hands so full of the troubles of reconstruction that it is doubtful if he gave a second thought to the "misdoings" in Utah, and Apostle Orson Pratt declared that Mormons intended "to live according to the law of God as we have received it, Congress or no Congress." Grant then had been President seven months. He settled the matter—not on the battlefield but in the courts.[17]

In summary, Grant was the "uncommon common man" in an age when the common man was coming into power. Longstreet warned Lee that Grant was "an all-round soldier, seldom if ever surpassed," and that "the biggest part of him" was his "pugnacious and plucky" heart.[18]

So the actors moved to their places, the drums rolled, and the curtain rose on the last act of national tragedy.

II

"A Jackass in the Original Package"

On the first day of February, 1864, frosty winds swept across the Potomac and skimmed the edges of the river with thin sheets of ice. Congressman Elihu B. Washburne, muffler wound around his throat, toiled up the hill to the Capitol with a good-humored countenance, for the prospect of a knockdown political fight warmed his blood like fine Madeira wine. The Congressman claimed Ulysses S. Grant "his by right of discovery," and after his "protégé's" military performances from Vicksburg (July 4, 1863) onward, Washburne proposed to revive the rank of lieutenant general for his Galena phenomenon.

Hitherto only George Washington and Winfield Scott had become lieutenant generals, so that conflicts of sentiment as well as of politics were involved in Washburne's suggestion. James Garfield of Ohio, who had fought with Grant and one day would occupy the White House, believed that if the rank were revived Grant would be converted into "a bureau officer in Washington," thus lessening his usefulness to the North. Indignantly General Addison Farnsworth of Illinois, a member of the Military Committee, emphasized that Grant was no "carpet-knight" and would never abandon a command in the field; and irascible Thad Stevens of Pennsylvania, who invariably talked with forked tongue upon any idea he opposed, slurringly commented, "Saints are not cannonized until after death."

According to Noah Brooks, a reporter and White House favorite, "Washburne . . . distinguished himself by the energy and impatience with which he fairly bulldozed the House." Insisting that the war could not end until Grant was raised to supreme command, Washburne bristled. "I can't wait. I want this now. Grant must fight out this war, and he will never leave the field!" [1]

Washburne carried the House by a vote of 86 to 41. Crossing his fingers, he agonized in silence as the resolution advanced to the Senate, where both friends and foes awaited the measure. At one extreme stood Jacob M. Howard of Michigan, who believed that the President "can have no ground whatever to complain . . . of the Senate in making this respectful request," and at the opposite extreme stood those radical Republicans who argued the bill was an insult to Lincoln by virtually saying, "Take our man or take the consequences." [2] When the Senate hassle ended on February 26, the measure passed and went to the White House for the President to sign or veto.

Danger still existed, as sly old Washburne well knew. He was not one, however, to leave any political stone unturned, especially in a presidential election year. The Congressman sensed with an almost undefined discomfiture the dim boom in the background to draft Grant as a nominee despite the General's avowal that after the war he wished only to be elected mayor of Galena and "have the sidewalk fixed up between my house and the depot." Politically, *Leslie's Weekly* had added to the delicacy of the situation by quipping, "If General Grant should go on joking in this dry style, he will soon joke Lincoln out of the next nomination." [3]

Washburne calculated the strongest defense. Unfortunately, Lincoln had never met Grant and even had neglected to send him a congratulatory note after he gave the Union its first major victory at Donelson, an unusual oversight on the President's part. The then Secretary of the Treasury, Salmon P. Chase of Ohio, a none-too-secret aspirant to the presidency, had complicated the issue by circulating the remarks of the explosive editor of the *Cincinnati Commercial*, Murat Halstead, when in 1863 Grant appeared hopelessly bogged down before Vicksburg: "Well, now, for God's sake say that Genl Grant, entrusted with our greatest army, is a jackass in the original package. He is a poor drunken imbecile. He is a poor stick sober, and he is most of the time more than half drunk, and much of the time idiotically drunk. . . ." [4]

"Honest Old Abe" acted in character, seeking truth in place of rumor. He asked Washburne to join Governor Richard Yates of Illinois and Adjutant General Lorenzo Thomas in ascertaining the facts. Lincoln's peppery Secretary of War, Edwin McMasters Stanton, trusting only those under his direct charge, dispatched his assistant secretary, Charles A. Dana, as a personal investigator. All four reported favorably upon Grant's military deportment, none more enthusiastically than Dana. So, in the end, whether or not those two Ohioans, Chase and Halstead, had embarked on a political conspiracy, the strategy backfired. Thereafter, to Washburne's delight, no matter how invidious the attacks upon Grant became, Lincoln stood stanchly behind Grant. The President, once satisfied, rarely changed his mind.

After the bill restoring the rank of lieutenant general appeared on the President's desk, the Congressman shrewdly suggested, almost offhandedly, that Lincoln should call to Washington some mutual friend like Russell Jones, United States Marshal of Illinois, who was completely informed concerning Grant's character and ambitions. The idea delighted Lincoln, to whom Jones was an old and intimate acquaintance, and no interview could have played more neatly into Washburne's schemes. Jones answered straightforwardly the President's numerous queries, then came directly to the crux of the matter: Did Grant seek the presidency?

"I confess I have a little curiosity on that point," Lincoln said.

Jones produced a private letter from Grant stating that he wished only for Lincoln to remain in office.

The President, gratified to the point of authorizing Grant's new commission, answered, "I wanted to know; for when this presidential grub once gets to gnawing at a man, nobody can tell how far in it has got. It is generally a good deal deeper than he himself supposes." [5]

Grant's growth in political knowledge was truly astonishing. While residing in St. Louis, he had joined the Know-Nothings, believing they were a social group, but he resigned immediately upon learning that he was associated with an antireligious, racist, political organization. No one knew whether he voted for Lincoln, in 1860 or in 1864. The reason why Grant later twice held the highest office in the land (and sorrowed when he was denied a bid for a third term) was due to the fact that the war placed him under the tutelage of some of the most astute politicians in America—among them Congressman Washburne, Secretary of War Stanton, and Senator John Sherman, the brother of General William Tecumseh Sherman.

Grant's ability to relate politics to the battlefield not only enhanced his attraction to Lincoln and Stanton but also identified him as the man of emerging military policies that would lead him, ultimately, to overwhelm Lee. Grant's idea of generalship was simply expressed: "When in doubt, fight"; and it was under this compulsion that for weeks in late 1863 he had pressed hard for permission to attack Mobile as a base for future operations in Mississippi, Alabama, and Georgia.

What favor this plan found in Washington depended on exerting a matching pressure on Lee in the East. Garfield's gossipy confidence to an old military crony, General William Starke Rosecrans, that both the President and the Secretary of War were "immensely disgusted with the late operations of the

Army of the Potomac" reflected bitterly upon General George Gordon Meade, its commander,[6] who had not capitalized upon his advantage in the East.

Stanton threw his hands upward in consternation at the thought of Meade, who impressed the Secretary as being continually "on the back track . . . without a fight." Dana and Stanton wracked their minds, seeking a successor for Meade. Sherman would be fine except that he was still needed in the West. They considered General William F. "Baldy" Smith, who as chief engineer of the Army of the Cumberland had rendered conspicuous service in saving Chattanooga. Momentarily, at least, "Baldy" should remain where he was. So, in the end, there was only Grant's star shining in the Union's military heavens. Grant would fight and, significantly to Stanton, agreed with Lincoln that if necessary colored troops should be used in crushing the Confederacy.[7] On Leap Year Day the Secretary wired Grant that his rank had been raised to lieutenant general. Three days later Stanton summoned Grant to Washington.

The man whose pen strokes scratched upon the register at Willard's, in early March, 1864, "U. S. Grant and son, Galena, Ill.," did not truly understand how far-reaching his fame had become, but his successes at Vicksburg and Chattanooga cast him in the role of being a general without equal in the North. Grant was now in his mid-forties and was scarcely a Beau Brummel in his "shabby-looking military suit," with a squint in his left eye and a wart on his right cheek. His shoulders were stooped, and the reddish tinge of his "bristling moustache" contrasted with his light brown hair. Almost everyone agreed that the General's very plainness drew people to him, for, in Margaret Leech's perceptive phrase, Grant was without "airs or falderols or highfalutin talk." [8]

Julia Grant, aware that 'Lyss tended to overdrink only when too long separated from his family, allowed their older boy to be his father's "conscience." In this function Fred Grant, fourteen years of age, was already a veteran who had been with his father at Donelson and Vicksburg and now accompanied the General into the dining room for a quick evening meal at Willard's. The youth grew acutely aware of the curious stares and whispers of the other diners. Suddenly one gentleman struck the tabletop with his knife, arose, and announced that the General was in the room. Cries of "Grant!" mixed with loud cheers. Fred saw his father rise and bow. The crowd surged around the table, and after "an informal reception" of perhaps forty-five minutes, Grant withdrew to his living quarters, unfed.

Later that night Senator Simon Cameron, the former Secretary of War, escorted Fred, the General, and his staff to the White House, where the last of the season's public receptions was being held. Lincoln strode across the room, held forth his hand, and cried, "I am most delighted to see you, General."

Lincoln beamed down eight inches upon the crown of Grant's head. The meeting left an indelible imprint upon Fred's memory. "I see them now before me, Lincoln, tall, thin and impressive, with deeply lined face, and his strong, sad eyes: Grant, compact, of good size . . . with his broad, square head and compressed lips—decisive and resolute. This was a thrilling moment, for in the hands of these two men was the destiny of our country. . . ." [9]

To Grant's aide, Horace Porter, Lincoln looked "more of a Hercules than an Adonis" in his ridiculously oversized collar and bizarrely broad necktie.[10] Lincoln, his adeptness at social amenities developed by four years in the White House, introduced Grant to Mrs. Lincoln and Secretary of State William H. Seward. Meanwhile White House visitors pressed nearer to catch a glimpse of the Union's "coming man," and Seward managed to pilot the General into the larger space of the East Room. Like a freak in a sideshow Grant was persuaded, with considerable reluctance, to stand upon a sofa so that all could see him.

Accounts thereafter vary. Porter thrilled to the cries of "Grant! Grant! Grant!" as "the vast throng" pushed forward to shake the General's hand. Noah Brooks's report was filled with journalistic fervor: "Ladies suffered dire disaster in the crush and confusion; their laces were torn and their crinolines mashed; and many got upon sofas, chairs, and tables to be out of harm's way or to get a better view of the spectacle." At least one man, Secretary of the Navy Gideon Welles, who was no Grant enthusiast, found the scene "rowdy and unseemly." [11]

Probably an hour passed before Grant escaped to a private room where the President waited.

Lincoln crossed his long legs and spoke soothingly to the exhausted Grant. The commission of lieutenant general, the President said, would be formally presented at one o'clock next day, March 9, 1864. The members of the Cabinet would attend. Probably Lincoln's eyes twinkled when he included his military adviser, Henry W. Halleck, a "book general" appropriately nicknamed "Old Brains," who almost had washed Grant out of the service in 1862 for reputed drunkenness and failure to report his intentions and whereabouts to headquarters. But, the President added quickly, as though balancing weights on a scale, Grant could bring the officers of his staff. Both Grant and he himself would speak briefly; understanding the other's shyness, Lincoln not only advised Grant to write his remarks but also suggested that he speak kindly of other generals, for both understood the possible jealousy which placing a Westerner in charge of the Army of the Potomac could arouse.

Grant returned the following afternoon, more ill at ease than he had been at his private meeting with the President. Welles, who viewed Grant as "destitute of originality," wrote years afterward that a "desultory conversation of half an hour took place." Others believed that Lincoln spoke graciously, calling Grant's new rank a mark of "the nation's appreciation of what you have done" and of its "reliance upon you for what remains to [be done]." Grant had difficulty in reading the notes he had scribbled in pencil on a half sheet of notepaper; he ignored both of the President's suggestions but did mutter politely that "it will be my earnest endeavor not to disappoint your expectations." Otherwise all Welles recalled of the occasion was the President's statement that the country wanted Grant to take Richmond and that Grant said "he could if he had the troops." [12] There was little sense discussing details until after Grant saw Meade regarding the condition of the Army of the Potomac and returned west to transfer his command there to Sherman.

Next day Grant, invited to dinner at the White House, declined with the blunt statement that he had "become very tired of this show business." [13] Already he had begun to react negatively to what Sherman called the "shams and ostentation" of the nation's capital. Apparently Grant read few newspapers— certainly not the *Washington Chronicle,* which announced that this evening the General would attend the performance at Grover's Theater where Edwin Booth, the country's leading tragedian, was playing a four-week engagement.

Grover's outdid itself for the occasion. Flags flamboyantly decorated the outside of the theater. Inside, from the box seats, hung banners inscribed with the names of Grant's battles. Disappointed and disgruntled Washingtonians, gazing at the ribbon across the front of the stage that spelled out "Unconditional Surrender" in gold letters, were learning that with Grant business came before pleasure.[14] At the moment he was in Meade's headquarters at Brandy Station, Virginia.

General Robert E. Lee refused to be stampeded into unsubstantiated conjectures over why Grant had come east. Possibly he intended to direct a campaign against Richmond, but on March 25 the General reminded Jefferson Davis that Northern newspapers often employed dubious or fictitious sources "to create false impressions."

Lee's magnificent generalship was based on the patience with which he analyzed the minutest detail of a military problem.

"Some hidden purpose," he warned the President, could have motivated these Northern stories. His mind posed the essential questions: Why would a commanding general announce when or to what place he was changing his headquarters? Why had Grant returned so hastily to the West? Might not Grant be up to some trickery similar to the "ruse . . . practiced at Vicksburg"? Davis remembered well Grant's strategy of transporting his army under the blazing guns of Vicksburg as though intending to invade some other port on the lower Mississippi; unexpectedly, Grant had swung back, driving his way between two armies and depriving Vicksburg of the reserves without which it could not be successfully defended.

A letter, dated March 23, from General John D. Imboden told Lee that troops were moving daily over the Baltimore & Ohio. "If true," Lee's mind reasoned, why should these men not be "recruits, convalescents & furloughed men going to the corps from the east now serving in the west, or they may be reinforcements for the [Confederate] Army of Tennessee?" Grant's next military movement, in Lee's opinion, should be against General Joseph E. Johnston, who was organizing forces around Dalton, Georgia, to assume an offense; or Grant could attack General James B. Longstreet, who threatened Knoxville. "The condition of the weather and the roads," Lee argued, "will probably be more favorable for active operations at an early day in the South than in Virginia where it will be uncertain for more than a month." [15]

West Pointers who fought both North and South had been schooled in the strategy and tactics of Baron (Antoine) Henri Jomini (1779–1869), a Swiss-born soldier who, fighting for France, first won distinction at Austerlitz and Jena (1805–06). To Jomini war followed a predictable pattern: "the objective, the offensive, mass, economy of force, interior lines, and unity of command." [16] Although Davis trusted Lee above all other generals, the President could not resist military meddling by dispersing his defense to check the enemy everywhere. Lee talked concentration against the enemy's main forces and wasted his breath in Richmond.[17] His command was restricted to the Army of Northern Virginia, which he named.

Very likely Grant was the least typical of the West Pointers on all the fields of battle. He had squandered countless hours at the Military Academy reading romantic novels and admitted that he had never studied Jomini. When as a colonel at the outset of the war Grant drilled troops, his commands were so awkward that to maneuver the men as he wished half the houses and all the fences in Springfield, Illinois, would have had to be torn down. Some men question if he ever studied a military textbook. He worked out his own style of campaigning. "The art of war is simple enough. Find out where your enemy is. Get at him as soon as you can. Strike at him as hard as you can and as often as you can, and keep on moving." [18] Soldiers said of their commander, "Old 'Lyss don't scare worth a damn."

On March 27, having completed consultations with George G. Meade and William Tecumseh Sherman, Grant returned to Washington. That evening he met at the War Department with President Lincoln, Secretary Stanton, and General Henry W. Halleck.[19]

On the second floor of Winder's Building two offices had been furnished for Grant as commanding general of all Union armies. His sense of feeling cramped was immediate. Let Halleck have the desk, carpeting, and proximity to the military telegraph in the War Department; Grant preferred a headquarters in the field near the Army of the Potomac, whence he could make as many "flying trips" to Washington as Lincoln wished.[20] A directness, a brusqueness, crept into the conversations between Grant and Lincoln, exemplified by the General's decision to bring from the West as his cavalry leader the youthful General Philip H. Sheridan. Even shorter than Grant and weighing only 115 pounds, "Little Phil" impressed the President as looking "worn down to almost a shadow by hard work." Was not Sheridan "rather a little fellow" to handle the cavalry? In a peppery mood, Grant replied, "You will find him big enough for the purpose when we get through with him." [21]

Legend has misled history in the claim that Lincoln brushed up on a knowledge of military science through books borrowed from the Library of Congress.[22] A respect for common sense drew the President to Grant, and how close the pair were in contriving plans to end the war was among the more important facts that Lee missed. Even Douglas Southall Freeman, the Virginian's most affectionate biographer, confessed that Lee rarely referred to Lincoln in conversation or correspondence. This indifference, perhaps Lee's only major shortcoming, was of vital momentary concern, for the "remarkable" Federal President by uniting with Grant "had now mustered all his resources of patience"; and, as spring of 1864 approached, those who "cunningly" sought to lead Lincoln were themselves led by him so that "his unconquerable spirit, in some mysterious manner, was being infused into the North." [23]

Later, writing a manuscript for the *North American Review*, Confederate General Richard Taylor, the son of former President Zachary Taylor, declared Grant had preferred assaulting Richmond via the James River but the Federal government insisted on an overland route that would place the Army of the Potomac between Lee's forces and Washington. If the government so persisted, Taylor quoted Grant as having said, his army "must be prepared for the additional loss of one hundred thousand men," which, Taylor continued, "were promised." Dour old Gideon Welles did not care how severely Taylor denigrated Grant (and the Union's Secretary of the Navy could have suggested ways of doing so), but there never had been any such offer, Welles declared, so that Taylor's charge became "a calumny on the humane, self-sacrificing, and lion-hearted Lincoln." [24]

Such waspish gossiping hindered Lee to the extent that he failed to grasp how Grant, with Lincoln's assistance, had created something Jefferson Davis's meddling never allowed Lee to achieve—Jomini's capstone of a unified system of command. How far afield this system could reach can only be appreciated by considering how little Davis permitted his generals to comprehend where the conflicting forces stood at the time Grant rose to lieutenant general. The Union guarded the Mississippi from St. Louis southward and held the line of the Arkansas, thus giving the Federals control of everything north of that river. The Union also claimed "a few points in Louisiana not remote from the river" as well as the mouth of the Rio Grande. East of the Mississippi, the North "held substantially" the country along the Memphis & Charleston Railroad as far as Chattanooga and the line of the Tennessee and Holston rivers, "taking in nearly all of the State of Tennessee." West Virginia was considered as belonging to the Union, in addition to that part of old Virginia north of the Rapidan and east of the Blue Ridge. Studying his maps of the seacoast, Grant could place marks of Federal power at Fortress (now Fort) Monroe and Norfolk in Virginia; at Plymouth, Washington, and New Bern in North Carolina; at Beaufort, Folly, and Morris islands and Hilton Head, Port Royal, and Fort Pulaski in South Carolina and Georgia; and at Fernandia, St. Augustine, Key West, and Pensacola in Florida. The balance of the South—"an empire in extent"—remained under the Confederate flag.[25]

Lincoln was an open-minded man, liking all classes of people and meeting them with candor and good humor. Thus, one Sunday morning, standing within the gates of the White House, he called out to a strange passer-by, "Good morning, good morning! I am looking for a newsboy; when you get to the corner I wish you would start one up this way."

Although far more reticent than the President, Grant was equally sensitive and fair in his personal dealings, as even that hypercritical group, the members of the press, could attest. A reporter who had written a slashing account of how Grant's soldiers had plundered a town was told by the General, "I simply want to say to you that if you always stick to the truth as you have here, we shall have no quarrel. The troops did behave very shamefully." [26]

Neither Lincoln nor Grant was very good at holding grudges or disguising personal feelings, factors that aided them enormously in creating their unified system of command. Halleck, who retained his dignity as Chief of Staff, would represent both Lincoln and Grant at Washington in coordinating dispatches and orders. Meade's offer to resign command of the Army of the Potomac touched Grant deeply. "It is men who wait to be selected, and not those who seek, from whom we may always expect the most efficient service." [27] In order that there could be no misunderstanding concerning Meade's authority, Grant established his headquarters at Culpeper, twelve miles nearer to Richmond than Meade's headquarters at Brandy Station.

The vastness of the Union's military establishment, with twenty departmental commanders all acting more or less independently, found Grant grumbling, "I determined to stop this." He reduced the number to seventeen. After three years of bloody battles from the James and Chickahominy near Richmond to Chambersburg and Gettysburg in Pennsylvania, the Army of the Potomac and the Army of Northern Virginia stood in about the same situation they had occupied in '61. Grant recalled, "I regarded the Army of the Potomac as the centre, and all west to Memphis along the line described as our position at the time, and north of it, the right wing; the Army of the James, under General [Benjamin F.] Butler, as the left wing, and all the troops south, as a force in rear of the enemy." [28]

Lincoln should have been fascinated to observe how Grant moved the pieces on his military chessboard. The IX Corps, over 20,000 troops under General Ambrose E. Burnside, rendezvoused at Annapolis, Maryland, where it could either act as a reinforcement to the Army of the Potomac or sail southward to menace coastal points in Virginia or North Carolina before

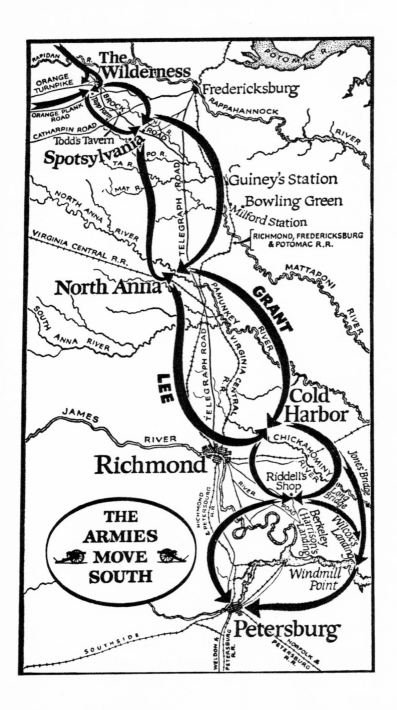

turning back on Richmond. Grant's instructions to Meade were the essence of simplicity: "Wherever Lee goes you will also go."

Grant passed his old command in the West to Sherman, then headquartered at Chattanooga, with orders to keep sharp watch on Johnston's military actions at Dalton, Georgia. Specifically, Sherman was to move against Johnston's army and break it up. Once Sherman plunged as far into the interior as he could, means must be found to inflict all possible damage upon the South's resources for waging war. As strongly as Grant could, he emphasized the fact that under no circumstance was a juncture to be allowed between the armies of Johnston and Lee.[29]

Grant planned three secondary operations: an attack on Mobile, in which the Navy was expected to cooperate; pressure upon Richmond from Fortress Monroe; and the devastation of "the granary of the South," as the Shenandoah Valley was then designated. Only the last of these movements was ever executed, and then at a much later date than Grant preferred; Admiral David G. Farragut, who had fought in the Navy before he reached teen age, captured Mobile in August, 1864.

During the difficult winter of 1863–64 Lee emerged as the fatherly, saintly image. Typical of the General was his Order No. 15, counseling the Army of Northern Virginia that "None but duties strictly necessary shall be required to be performed on Sunday, and that all labor, both of men and animals, which it is practicable to anticipate or postpone, or the immediate performance of which is not essential to the safety, health, or comfort of the army, shall be suspended on that day."

Even inspections by commanding officers were to be planned for a time that would "not interfere with the attendance of the men on divine service at the customary hour in the morning." [30]

Few were those who knew that Lee first suffered from "rheumatic pains" in 1863. That winter his physical "incapacities" increased. Acute pericarditis added to his first complaint of the war. His face was florid, and he could not conceal the hypertension which, combined with angina pectoris, finally carried him to the grave.[31]

In these months of silent suffering the Virginian became the "noble Lee," who liked to live with his troops in wet weather or dry, warm weather or cold, and to share the same food ration as they. He knew that cotton exchanged for the supplies of victuals and clothing so desperately needed by his men could fall into enemy hands, but in a mid-February letter to James A. Seddon, the Confederate Secretary of War, Lee believed the risk worth taking, for "if the Government will send 100,000 pounds of those yarns to New Market they can readily be exchanged at the rate of one pound of cotton for two of cured bacon." [32] Numerous letters home thanked the women of Richmond for knitting stockings for his neglected soldiers, and the Lee home in Richmond was described as "an industrial school" where everyone was busy plying their knitting needles. Somewhat querulously, one letter from the General to his wife pointed out that two pairs were missing from the twenty-five she had said were enclosed.

Where Lee differed from Davis was in his adaptability. The President wanted the war to stay fixed, as he saw it, which of course it would not. As an excellent Southern historian, Clifford Dowdey, has written, "To continue [Davis's] policy of dispersed defenses, on whatever theory, became unrelated to reason." But Davis could not yield his preconceived notion. "In this he was like any individual caught in a supreme sequence of personal failures, who can only repeat over and over what worked, or seemed to work, before." [33]

Lee tactfully must live with the truth; Davis in the Mexican War had never led anything stronger than a volunteer regiment. In no military sense was he Lee's equal. The fact that Lee could understand so clearly Grant's objective as early as April 7 was revealed in a letter to Davis's chief military adviser, General Braxton Bragg: "I think every preparation should be made to meet the approaching storm, which will apparently burst on

Virginia. . . ." [34] That same day Lee acted on his military
instincts by issuing a circular to his troops:

I hope that few of the soldiers of this army will find it necessary at
any time in the coming campaign to surrender themselves prisoners of
war. We cannot spare brave men to fill Federal prisons. Should, however, any be so unfortunate as to fall through unavoidable necessity
into the hands of the enemy, it is important that they should preserve
entire silence with regard to everything connected with the army, the
positions, movements, organizations, or probable strength of any portion of it. I wish the commanding officers of regiments and companies
to instruct their men, should they be captured, under any circumstances not to disclose the brigade, division, or corps to which they
belong, but to give simply their names, company, and regiment, and
not to speak of military matters even among their associates in misfor-
tune. Proper prudence on the part of all will be of great assistance in
preserving that secrecy so essential to success.[35]

On this same day Longstreet's corps, then stationed at Bristol
where the boundary line of Virginia and Tennessee divides the
main thoroughfare, was ordered to Charlottesville to await
further instructions from Lee. The rumored number of troops
the Union was mustering to throw against Virginia was obviously
alarming, and doubtless, for all the courage of his remark, anxiety
edged Lee's voice when he told a staff aide, Walter H. Taylor,
"Colonel, we have got to whip them; we must whip them, and
it has already made me better to think of it." [36]

Generally, British military critics compare Lee and Grant to
the latter's disadvantage. The British analysts were, on the whole,
drawn to the Virginian's aristocratic posture, which appealed
so strongly to their romantic natures, and to his Jominian background in war, which did not overstrain their conservative minds.
When Grant was ridiculed for a style of fighting that amounted
to "hard pounding," his critics unwittingly repeated a phrase
that belonged to the Duke of Wellington; Grant's own term
was "continuous pounding," which was quite another matter:

Insofar as the contest between Lee and Grant was the greatest civil war spectacle up to that time in either the Old World or New, it deserves to have the contrasting characters of its principal actors clearly defined. A profound student of war, British General J. F. C. Fuller, has recognized the conflict of personalities between Grant and Lee and has delineated them handsomely. Where Lee paused, Grant did not possess the "imagination" to do so; where Lee trusted in God, Grant relied upon "big battalions." So the drama about to unfold also had a plot to Fuller: "It was [for Lee] a struggle between hope and faith, resistance against pressure, imagination against logic, and behind it all—a moribund cause battling with a virile one." [37]

Lee was "something parochial" and Grant "something cosmic," in Fuller's estimation. As a result, Lee, pursuing the "most skilful, masterful and heroic" campaign of his career, ended in tragedy:

Lee was confronted not only by a man he could not understand, but by a problem and a war which were utterly novel to him. He had been fighting generals [such as McClellan on the Peninsula, Pope at Second Manassas, Hooker at Chancellorsville, Burnside at Fredericksburg] who lacked direction, and who had no conception of how to win peace; who, possessing little or no strategy, floundered through a tactical gloom, only to be derided by the politicians who should have supported them.

Grant's advantage was in bringing his own strategy with him from the West, and once the President understood Grant's objective, "Lincoln stood like a rock" behind his lieutenant general. A tragedy, once begun, must run its course. Its dimensions became awesome. "Not a day's, or a two, or even a three days', engagement," Fuller explained, "but a relentless tussle of weeks and months." [38]

III

Lee Leaves
the Mountain

Apple blossoms sweetened the air in the orchards around Washington. A sense of reviving life filled the approaching spring, for throughout the North the people believed that with Grant in Virginia the war must soon end. Within the Army of the Potomac opinions differed. A common level may have been struck by the Maine officer who said that "after the debonair McClellan, the cocky Burnside, rosy Joe Hooker, and the dyspeptic Meade, the calm and unpretentious Grant was not exciting." [1] Meade's aide, Colonel Theodore Lyman, found in the Lieutenant General, who possessed "somewhat the air of a Yankee schoolmaster," not only "a good deal of rough dignity" but also "an expression as if he had determined to drive his head through a brick wall." In this "lull before the hurricane, which little short of a miracle can avert," Lyman saw Grant as "all big with strategy" who intended "to do something pretty serious before he gives up." [2]

Washington A. Roebling—who would achieve the engineering marvel of his age by completing the construction of the Brooklyn Bridge, designed by his father—was not an altogether unprejudiced witness. "Wash" was in love with the sister of General Gouverneur K. Warren, in whose corps he served, and was suspicious of any interloper from the West who might challenge the military judgment of his future brother-in-law. Lyman saw Wash as "the most immovable of men" who went "poking about in the most dangerous places . . . with an air of entire indifference," [3] and Roebling's over-all respect in the army perhaps permitted him to ridicule the western import as "Useless Grant." Wash described a scene at Culpeper when another Westerner, the President, "mounted on a hard-mouthed, fractious horse," reviewed the troops:

"Soon after the march began his hat fell off; next, his pantaloons, which were not fastened on the bottom, slipped up to his knees, showing his white, home-made drawers secured below with some white tape, which presently unraveled and slipped up also, revealing a long, hairy leg." [4]

General Robert McAllister, a Scotch Presbyterian warrior who served in the 11th New Jersey Infantry and was known as "Mother" McAllister for the gentle solicitude he lavished upon his soldiers, drew a temperate view of Grant, who could become so absorbed in his own thoughts that "he often forgot to return the salute of passing officers." The fact that Grant had the "secret of keeping his own secrets" impressed McAllister as "a good thing for the success of our cause." McAllister witnessed a scene familiar whenever a campaign impended: "I rode up on a little bluff; and as I reached the summit, I heard a voice. On looking down into a stone quarry I saw two of our boys earnestly engaged in prayer. I turned away as quietly as possible, thinking how delightful it was to find such deep religious feeling in my regiment. . . ." [5]

Grant had approximately eight weeks after his appointment as lieutenant general to plan a coordinated campaign, east and west. Critics of Grant often miss the point that he intended for four armies to move simultaneously: Meade's, Butler's at Fortress Monroe, another under Franz Sigel in the Shenandoah, and Sherman against Joseph E. Johnston in the West. The Southern cause was waning, the Confederacy's desertions increasing. Grant's objective in Virginia was to destroy Lee's army, and although he recognized that the Wilderness was "a natural outwork protecting Richmond on its northern flank," Grant decided to move by the left—that is, against or around Lee's right—a maneuver Fuller defends as "strategically sound" even if "the Wilderness was the worst possible area to fight in." Already Lee had "gobbled up" Burnside and Hooker because they had failed to penetrate the Wilderness, but Grant accepted the situation with an easygoing philosophy: as long as he must fight Lee, "it was better to fight him outside of his stronghold [Richmond] than in it." [6] He wished that he could replace Butler with Baldy Smith, but insofar as this was an election year and Lincoln must rely on Butler's considerable political influence in Massachusetts, Grant withdrew that request with philosophical equanimity.[7]

At least Grant could take comfort in the quality of his corps commanders, as William Swinton, one of the first and in many respects best historians of the Army of the Potomac, emphasized:

The three corps commanders [corps designated as the II, V, and VI] were men of a high order of ability, though of very diverse types of character. [General Winfield Scott] Hancock [II Corps] may be characterized as the ideal of a *soldier*: gifted with a magnetic presence and a superb personal gallantry, he was one of those lordly leaders who, upon the actual field of battle, rule the hearts of troops with a potent and irresistible mastery. Warren [in whose V Corps Wash Roebling served] owed his promotion to the signal proofs of ability he had given, first as a brigadier, then as chief-engineer of the army, and latterly as the temporary commander of the Second Corps.[8] Of a subtle, analytic intellect, endowed with an eminent talent for details, the clearest military *coup d'oeil*, and a fiery concentrated energy, he promised to take the first rank as a commander. [General John] Sedgwick, long the honored chief of the Sixth Corps, was the exemplar of the steadfast soldierly obedience to duty: singularly gentle and child-like in character, he was scarcely more beloved in his own command than throughout the army.[9]

Grant's mind was decided. On April 29 he wrote Halleck, who was now the liaison man between Stanton and Lincoln:

My own notions about our line of march are entirely made up, but as circumstances beyond my control may change them, I will only state that my effort will be to bring Butler's and Meade's forces together.

The army will start with fifteen days' supplies; all the country affords will be gathered as we go along. This will no doubt enable us to go twenty or twenty-five days without further supplies, unless we should be forced to keep in the country between Rapidan and the Chickahominy, in which case supplies might be required by way of the York or the Rappahannock Rivers. . . . When we get once established on the James River there will be no further necessity of occupying the road south of Bull Run.[10]

If a siege of Richmond developed, a note told Meade, "siege guns, ammunition, and equipments can be got from the arsenals at Washington and Fort Monroe." [11]

On this April 29, while Grant wrote to Halleck, Lee left his headquarters at Orange Court House to visit the returning I Corps under Longstreet. "Old Pete," as this general was affectionately called, was pleasantly settled near Gordonsville. Longstreet's adventure to the West had thinned his ranks to no more than 10,000 men, yet they cheered Lee as though twice that number, and, as one veteran remarked, "Our clothes were patched and brushed up, so far as was in our power, boots and shoes greased, the tattered and torn old hats were given here and there 'a lick and a promise,' and on the whole I must say I think we presented not a bad-looking body of soldiers." Lee smiled back, most likely with a twitch of the heart.[12]

That same heart twitch must have followed when at the month's end Lee visited his signal station on Clark's Mountain. Through his glasses he beheld an unhappy scene as he searched the valley of the Rapidan. Fields that should have grown grain were now neglected. Soldiers had torn down fences and barns for winter campfires. What livestock that had not been eaten had been removed to the rear. Lee asked Sergeant B. L. Wynn, in charge of the station, if a watch was kept at night.

"No," Wynn answered.

"Well, you must put one on," Lee said.

Disturbing reports reached Lee from these nighttime vigils. The columns of smoke rising from the north bank of the Rapidan grew denser. Moving lights were visible in the dark, and daylight revealed the dust of marching Federal columns. Gray-coated soldiers sent to the rear the "luxuries" of winter: a fiddle, a chessboard, a set of quoits; they grumbled over Northern newspaper reports that the sutler wagons they had planned on plundering had been ordered by Grant to leave his army; yet they remained cheerful although they had heard the rumors that they might be outnumbered two to one in the coming engagement.[13]

Lee was undecided whether Grant would move on the Confederate right toward Fredericksburg or by the Confederate left toward Gordonsville. His reliance was on God, Lee told Davis, "But . . . I must have provisions and forage." The Virginian was not overawed by either Grant or his superior numbers, saying, "I have no uneasiness as to the result of the campaign in Virginia." On the morning of May 2 Lee returned to Clark's Mountain. This time, as he studied the Federal positions, he could answer all questions but one. Grant obviously intended to plunge into the Wilderness, but would he cross the river at Ely's Ford or Germanna?[14]

Lee came down from the mountain and ordered a three-day ration for the troops. As he wrote R. E. Lee, Jr., the Army of Northern Virginia was ready for whatever the Almighty ordained.

On the night of May 3–4, signalmen on Clark's Mountain reported to Lee that troops could be seen marching past the glow of Federal campfires. The task of moving an army in excess of 100,000 men was an enormous undertaking, for it involved transporting as well 4,300 wagons, the artillery, 835 ambulances, 33,991 public and private horses, and 22,258 mules. Andrew A. Humphreys, Meade's chief of engineers, provided canvas bridges which were retrieved after the men had crossed the Rapidan.

Although the Union forces approached that "mining region, the home of the whip-poor-will and the bat and the owl" known as the Wilderness, Grant did not wish to fight Lee here. The Army of the Potomac was by now thoroughly familiar with this country where the many creeks and rivulets flowed through oak-covered ridges and knolls. Sweet gum, cedar, and pine trees barely raised their tops above the dense undergrowth. Ravines and tangled thickets could be traversed only along "winding cow-paths." Lieutenant Colonel Adam Badeau, who served Grant as military secretary, understood that a battle here must become "a wrestle as blind as midnight"; Swinton compared the place to a "hell-cauldron." [15]

Grant had hoped to avoid meeting Lee in the Wilderness; he needed open ground for his superior numbers to tip the balance in the Union's favor. Humphreys thought Grant might succeed, for the troops were in excellent condition and "were quite equal to, and ready for, a continuous march of thirty miles or more in twenty-four hours," in which case they would be "substantially clear of the Wilderness." [16]

Lee, who would take any risk to conserve his 64,000 effectives, had no intention of allowing Grant to meet him anywhere but in the Wilderness. A shrewd flanking movement by the Virginian threatened to place the Army of Northern Virginia between Hancock's II Corps and Warren's V. On the morning of May 4, Meade, Warren, and Sedgwick met at the Old Wilderness Tavern and decided they must attack the Rebels without waiting for Hancock. Along the lines of Sedgwick's VI Corps ran the cry, "Forward! by the right flank; forward!" An unidentified veteran described the scene that followed:

Through a thicket, blind and interminable; over abattis of fallen trees; through swamps, and ditches, and brush-heaps; and once—a glorious breathing-space—across a half acre of open field, the obedient troops move on. . . . Sometimes the eyes of the men sink to note a by-path in the forest, like that which many a one has travelled in old days to some old spring of homelike memory. And here is the "birr" of a bullet, like that which startled one who heard it one summer afternoon, when a brother hunter was careless, and fired at a partridge as he stood in range. The bee-like sounds are thicker on the ridge; in the forest, a little way ahead, there is a crackling, roaring tumult, seasoned with wild cheers.

The warming morning sun beat down on this sixteen or seventeen square miles of the Wilderness that lay between Fredericksburg and Orange Court House. The number of regiments, Union and Confederate, increased, as Sedgwick's unidentified veteran resumed his report:

The fighting—who shall describe it? Not a thousand men can be seen at once, yet for miles in the front thousands are engaged. The volleyed thunders of the combat roll among the glens and ravines hoarser and higher than the voices of an Eastern jungle. The woods are alive with cries and explosions, and the shrill anvil-clatter of musketry. One cannon, pitched afar, times the wild tumult like a tolling bell. The smoke is a shroud about our heroes; there is not wind enough to lift it into a canopy.

And now, out of the concealed and awful scenery where the fight goes on, there come the ruins it has wrought, in shapes borne in blankets and on litters—maimed, tortured, writhing; with eyes dull with the stupor of coming death, or bright with delirious fire. Listen to the hell raging beyond and below; behold this silent, piteous procession, that emerges carelessly, and passes on. . . .

At two o'clock a quiet settled upon the Wilderness. But Hancock had come up now—the lull did not last long. By four o'clock Hancock commanded half of the army in action. Then, judging the sound of the shock of battle from left to right:

Hancock is advancing. Sedgwick is advancing, Warren is in partial wait. Along the left a guttural, oceanic roar prevails, without an interval of rest. Like a great engine, dealing death, the Second corps and its supports move forward, taking equal death in return.

Companies, regiments, brigades melt away. At most, a half mile of ground is gained.[17]

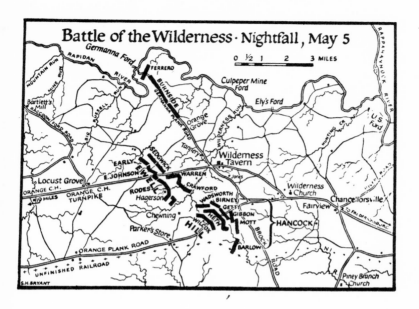

Battle of the Wilderness · Nightfall, May 5

Some of the events of the day's fighting seemed unbelievable in retrospect. General McAllister that evening "found the bones of our dead laying and bleaching on top of the ground." Trees were cut to pieces. Sleep became impossible. McAllister's New Jersey 11th had marched twenty-five miles before reaching the Wilderness at Chancellorsville, and those who tired quickest had "indulged the most freely in commissary whiskey during the winter." Among the more lurid relics "was a skull, the cap still upon it, and upon the visor was stamped 'D. Bender, Co. H, 11th N.J. Vols.'" McAllister sent his wife a different kind of trophy—"two or three pretty violets and flowers" picked on the battlefield. The ground where they grew had become "rich by the blood of our brave soldiers."

"I thought the flowers would be a relick [sic] prised [sic] by you," McAllister wrote.[18]

Colonel Lyman saw Grant sitting on the grass, puffing a briarwood pipe and "looking sleepy and stern and indifferent."

Meade ordered his aide to find Hancock, who had come up at 4:15 P.M. The musketry of Hancock's forces could be heard on the left, and Meade wanted periodic reports until nightfall ended the battle. Rifle fire crashed in the woods in Lyman's front, and all too often stray balls were landing nearby. The scene, Lyman thought, was "all very well for a novel," but at the moment he preferred to be elsewhere. Yet he found Hancock and was treated to an intimate glimpse of a corps commander in action:

"Report to General Meade," said Hancock, "that it is very hard to bring up troops in this wood, and that only a part of my Corps is up, but I will do as well as I can." Up rides an officer: "Sir! General [George W.] Getty is hard pressed and nearly out of ammunition." "Tell him to hold on and General [John] Gibbon will be up to help him." Another officer: "General [Gershom] Mott's division [in which McAllister served] has broken, sir, and is coming back." "Tell him to stop them, sir!!" roared Hancock in a voice of a trumpet. As he spoke, a crowd of troops came from the woods and fell back into the Brock road. Hancock dashed among them. "Halt here! Halt here! Form behind this rifle-pit. Major [William G.] Mitchell, go to Gibbon and tell him to come up on the double-quick!" It was a welcome sight to see [Samuel S.] Carroll's brigade coming along that Brock road, he riding at their head as calm as a May morning. "Left face—prime— forward," and the line disappeared in the woods to waken the musketry with double violence. Carroll was brought back wounded. Up came [Alexander] Hays's brigade, disappeared in the woods, and, in a few minutes, General Hays was carried past me, covered with blood, shot through the head.[19]

The day's fight had amounted to Indian warfare and the results were indecisive, even though the firing continued after darkness. The affair added up to what Grant had expected. Certainly he was in no mood to listen to a rumor that Lee was about to worm his way between the Rapidan and the Army of the Potomac, thus cutting it off completely from its communications.

Grant's temper snapped. He rose from a campstool and

removed a freshly lighted cigar. "Oh, I am heartily tired of hearing about what Lee is going to do," he declared. "Some of you always seem to think he is suddenly going to turn a double somersault, and land in our rear and on both of our flanks at the same time. Go back to your command, and try to think what we are going to do ourselves, instead of what Lee is going to do." [20]

IV

"When Lincoln Kissed Me"

John Cheves Haskell, who fought with Longstreet, heard the distant rumble of the first day's fighting in the Wilderness. "Old Pete" Longstreet drove his corps on an all-night march to reinforce Lee. The stump of a right arm that Haskell retained from the Peninsula Campaign in '62 twinged in the chill of darkness. About daylight on May 6 Longstreet called his troops to take to the double-quick, and two hours later they reached the plank road from Fredericksburg to Orange Court House.

Haskell, as a Carolinian, could speculate on those prewar days when almost everyone "had gone wild on secession." There had been prayers that Lincoln would be elected, making war inevitable. Haskell was with a group of college friends on the night Lincoln's election became certain; giddy-headed, they rushed to Hunt's Hotel in Columbia, South Carolina, where F. J. Moses, a lawyer from Sumter, made "a most violent secession speech" intended to arouse "the weak-kneed and hesitating."

Haskell had fought for the Confederacy from the outbreak of the war and believed that he had learned everything about the savagery of this far from glamorous profession. Within a few short hours he would be taught a different lesson.[1]

The awakening toward which Haskell advanced began that day

when Hancock renewed his attack upon A. P. Hill's brigades along the Orange Plank Road.[2] Lyman, who was in the saddle by five o'clock that morning, found a smiling Hancock at a road crossing.

"We are driving them, sir," Hancock said. "Tell General Meade we are driving them most beautifully. [General David B.] Birney has gone in and he is just cleaning them out bea-u-ti-fully!"

Lyman welcomed the receding line of musketry and "those infernal minié balls." But the colonel brought discouraging news. "I am ordered to tell you, sir, that only one division of General Burnside is up, but that he will go in as soon as he can be put in position."

Hancock answered vehemently. "I knew it! Just what I expected. If he could attack *now*, we would smash A. P. Hill all to pieces!" [3]

Not too long after Hancock burst into this outrage, Haskell reached the field of battle. Men from Hill's corps rushed through the lines Longstreet endeavored to form. They cried that the Yankees were "in enormous force," and Haskell, realizing they were "utterly panic-stricken," feared that the result might be "a headlong stampede." But Longstreet, "always grand in battle," stemmed the retreat.

"Longstreet," said Haskell, "rode up and down the lines, encouraging, exhorting, and steadying the men, with an effect on them that no other leader I ever saw had on his troops. In a short time he had the line straightened out and steadied, with the men pouring volley after volley into the enemy, who were only a short distance away."

Often no more than a hundred yards separated friend from foe. Shots scarred the scrub oak saplings. Horsemen tried not to ride over their own wounded but could not avoid this tragedy. "It looked," Haskell wrote, "as if no human being could stand under such sheets of fire as were flashing back and forth." [4]

The spirit Longstreet had infused into his corps was revealed in the jeers and laughter they bestowed upon their retreating comrades in arms.

"Do you belong to Lee's Army?" veterans taunted as Longstreet organized his front line.[5]

To Haskell, Old Pete was "the greatest fighter and tactician" the war had produced, especially after the Union troops, crumbling with increasing rapidity, "left the field routed." Longstreet ordered Haskell to bring up a battery on the plank road and rake the woods on either side. As the Confederates advanced, Haskell saw in the "dust and heat" the dying Union General James S. Wadsworth, shot through the head. Captured Yankees called the New Yorker "a very brave man."

A pause followed, required for straightening the lines again and bringing up ammunition. In this interim Longstreet conferred briefly with Lee, General Micah Jenkins of South Carolina, and General William ("Little Billy") Mahone of Virginia. The Federals continued to give ground under Longstreet's pressure.

Jenkins had fought brilliantly and was jubilant as Longstreet rode near his column. Thinking of the promotion that must surely result, he called on the men of his brigade to cheer Longstreet. The gray cloth worn by Jenkins's men was so dark as to appear black. Haskell described the tragedy that resulted:

Mahone's men, some distance off in the thick underbush, hearing the cheers and seeing this body of dark uniformed men, took them for Yankees and fired a volley. Fortunately they fired high, or there would have been a terrible slaughter. As it was, while they only struck eight or ten mounted men, the effect was horrible, for among the few were Jenkins, shot through the head, and Longstreet, shot through the neck.

Both men fell. The gritty Longstreet, whose right arm had been paralyzed by the shot, crawled forward, waving his left hand to Mahone's troops, who now realized, "horror-stricken," what had occurred. Lee was told, and came to the scene, but time was consumed, the Union forces recovered from their "panic," the Confederates "moved forward in a feeble-hearted way," and, Haskell concluded, "the chance which we had never had before and were never to have again was lost." [6]

Confederate General Moxley Sorrel, as invariably happens with eyewitnesses, saw the situation differently, yet he praised Long-street unstintingly as a "fighting soldier" when Hancock fell upon the "unprepared divisions" of Henry Heth and Cadmus Wilcox in Hill's III Corps, and before Longstreet arrived Sorrel believed "it looked as if things were past mending." Lee was "under great excitement" on the left, because the Texas Brigade would not fight until Lee had retired for his own self-protection. Longstreet's arrival helped Lee "to regain his calm," and, fighting with three brigades on each side of the road, Sorrel said, "we went in earnest." [7]

Lyman, who believed "they know everything, those Rebels," credited Longstreet with full knowledge of Burnside's tardiness in reinforcing Hancock. Thereafter, once the Rebels struck, a promised victory turned into a threatened defeat.[8]

As the Federals fell back, Colonel Theodore Lyman drew his sword and tried to rally them at a rifle pit, but his efforts were wasted. He was especially exasperated by a German color-bearer, "a stupid, scared man."

"Jeneral Stavenzon [Stevenson]," he said, "he telled me for to carry ze colors up ze road."

Lyman threatened to run his sword through the fellow if he did not plant the colors on the rifle pit, but the German plodded stoically to the rear. Burnside's extravagant convolutions in march-ing and countermarching finally ended at two o'clock, when he did attack. Hancock's men were all along the road, "but regiments and brigades were all mixed up," and Hancock had no alternative but merely to listen to Burnside fighting.[9] An eyewitness said:

About this battle there is a horrible fascination. It is like a mael-strom. You feel it sucking you in and you go nearer to see men fall like those you have seen fallen. Down through the break, underneath the edges of the smoke, where the bullets are thick and the trunks of trees, like the ranks of men, sway and fall with the smiting of shells, you have a little view of the courage and the carnage of this fight. There are the enemy, retreated to the breastworks—a ragged pile of fallen trees and heaped-up earth—hiding their heads, spitting lead and

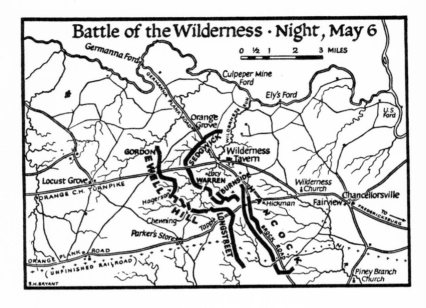

flame. Here is the Sixth Corps—what you can see of it—plunging on, firing continually, tumbling over branches and limbs, sinking waist deep in swamps, fighting with its might and bleeding at every pore. The troops of the First division, under [General Horatio G.] Wright, are martyred for a time in a ravine swept by musketry in front, and by a crossfire of artillery from right and left. The few guns that we have posted to the left have funeral voices for our enemy on the ridge, perishing beneath their fire in scores. The ridge is taken, the division breathes once more, but on come the enemy, an avalanche of greater numbers, pushing us back. . . .[10]

Remembering the night of May 7, Sergeant Thomas D. Marbaker, who served with McAllister in the 11th New Jersey Volunteers, told how the Federals started down the "Meade and Lee express route" to move nearer Richmond. Marbaker was strangely affected by that night march through "the gloom of the forest, so deep as to be almost shadowless . . . clumps of bushes, stumps and fallen limbs took weird and threatening shapes . . . logs became lurking foes . . . and, reaching down, our hands perhaps would fall upon the clammy face of a corpse, for the woods was filled with death's ghastly trophies." [11]

Wash Roebling was disenchanted by every phase of the two-day battle in the Wilderness. He was not an unprejudiced witness, because he believed that Lynchburg rather than Richmond should have been Grant's objective in outflanking Lee, certainly a debatable surmise. But Wash criticized Grant on many points:

First, on Grant's "fatuous assumption" that Lee would be "afraid to attack him" and his sending Hancock toward Bowling Green beyond Todd's Tavern "with ⅓ the best troops of the army"; second, for Grant's "failure to seize the high open commanding ground on the plank road"; and third, for "the failure of Meade or Grant to appear personally at the vital part of the Battlefield." Wrote Wash, "One glance in the morning would have shown them that the occupation of the plank road would have been half the battle won." No enemy, Wash claimed, was then in sight.

However, Wash could not avoid giving away his own prejudice when he explained why no veteran ever visited the site of the conflict since "after a lapse of 20 or 40 years a Virginia battle field becomes utterly unrecognizable" because "houses are gone and new ones have sprung up."

Still, memories did not fade that quickly, and Wash could never forget how his future brother-in-law, General Warren, had received from Grant a "peremptory order" that unless Warren "instantly attacked" in the underbrush where General Samuel W. Crawford then stood, Grant would *"cashier [Warren] on the spot."* The italics, like the bitterness, belonged to Wash.[12]

Gossips in Washington sometimes declared that Grant disliked Halleck and Stanton. Halleck said "bosh." Stanton called stories of quarrels with Grant "gratuitous lies" and, clearing the record, snapped, "Grant quarrels with no one." But as two days passed without word of what was happening to Grant in the Wilderness, an assistant noticed Stanton's hand tremble as he reached for a paper. An anxious President joined Stanton and Halleck in pacing the floor of the telegraph room in the War Department.[18]

Generally, newspaper correspondents in the Wilderness "moved through the bedlam as if in a dream." The countryside was reported overrun by Major John S. Mosby's Confederate guerrillas, rendering hopeless any attempt to reach Washington. Representatives of the *New York Herald* and *New York World* offered $1,000 to anyone willing to risk the journey northward. There were no takers.

But Henry E. Wing, a "loner" working his first assignment for the *New York Tribune*, convinced Grant that he really expected to get to Washington. Standing with a hand on the young man's shoulder, Grant gave him a personal message for the President.

At four in the morning Wing set out to find a Unionist friend near Ely's Ford. Wing never would escape Mosby's guard, the friend said, unless he dressed as a Confederate courier carrying news of a great Lee victory of importance to influential Confederate sympathizers in Washington. Wing changed into "a butternut suit, a pair of coarse brogans, and a dilapidated hat of quilted cotton."

In this disguise the *Tribune* man succeeded in crossing the Rapidan, but one of his guerrilla guides, a hardened one-armed secessionist named Kelly, grew suspicious when they reached the bluff of the Rappahannock and could hear the far-off rumble of battle. Wing did not linger to argue the point but plunged into the river while bullets hissed around him. Reaching the opposite shore with his horse, Wing felt fairly safe but almost immediately ran into another band of guerrillas picking up stores abandoned by the troops marching toward the Wilderness.

Wing parted from his horse and hid in a clump of bushes until the scavengers had departed. There was naught for the reporter to do now but walk. Toward dusk he reached Manassas Junction and hid there until nightfall, when he hobbled along the tracks of the Orange & Alexandria Railroad. A Federal picket captured him at a point where a trestle crossed Bull Run and led him to post headquarters at Union Mills. Here, luckily, Wing was recognized.[14]

The President could admire the blossoming trees of early May and put off the overinquisitive by joking that Grant had entered the Wilderness "and pulled the hole in after him," but an acquaintance like George Templeton Strong of the Sanitary Commission realized how haggard "Uncle Abraham" appeared. Lincoln was with Stanton when the telegraph began clicking with a message from Union Mills. Wing addressed Charles A. Dana, Assistant Secretary of War, requesting permission to use the military telegraph to send a story to the *Tribune*. "I am just in from the front," Wing wired. "Left Grant at four o'clock this morning."

Stanton demanded to know where the reporter had left Grant. Wing wired that he would tell nothing before sending a hundred words to his paper. Stanton repeated his unilateral demand, but the *Tribune* man stood by his original proposition. Stanton, "wild with anxiety," ordered Wing arrested. In after years the reporter wrote, "Of course that settled it. I would not have told him one little word to save my life."

Lincoln, unlike Stanton, did not believe in threats. The President sent his own message to Union Mills. Said the operator to Wing, now sleepily stretched out on a bench, "Mr. Lincoln wants to know if you will tell *him* where Grant is." Wing repeated his first proposition, which the President immediately accepted, "only suggesting that my statement . . . disclose to the public the general situation." Lincoln also wanted a summary sent to the Associated Press.

On May 7 Wing was brought to Washington in the cab of a "special locomotive." He arrived sometime around 2 A.M. A carriage waited to rush him to the White House. Although Wing told all he knew, occasionally pointing out a place of engagement on a map on the wall, the sum of the account as Lincoln and his "anxious" cabinet members analyzed it was that both armies had suffered terribly. The reporter added that he brought a special message from Grant.

"He told me to tell you, Mr. President," Wing said, "that there would be no more turning back."

A delighted Lincoln threw his arms around the reporter and kissed him, giving Wing the title for a future book: *When Lincoln Kissed Me: A Story of the Wilderness Campaign.*[15] At a Marine Band concert on the grounds of the White House that night, Lincoln, appearing on the portico, proposed "In lieu of a speech" that "we give three cheers for Major [Lieutenant] General Grant and all the armies under his command."[16]

V

"On to Richmond!"

It is doubtful that there was ever such a battle as had been waged on May 5 and 6 in the "gloomy woods" of the Wilderness, a battle "horrible, yet fascinating," a battle shrouded in mystery which "no man could see, and whose progress could only be followed by the ear." [1] The combat ended at night with the woods aflame and choking smoke everywhere—"war in Inferno"—"and from the thickets came the cries of the wounded, frantic lest the flames reach them ere the litter-bearers did." [2] Sitting under a pine tree, Grant removed his briarwood pipe and told Colonel Lyman in a cool voice, "Tonight Lee will be retreating South." But Grant was wrong; Lee believed that there would be at least one more day of heavy fighting. Beyond a desultory exchange of picket fire, however, May 7 passed peaceably. From the Confederate left came a report that Union troops had begun to move.

For Lee this news posed the question of whither Grant would turn: eastward toward Fredericksburg or southeastward toward Richmond through Spotsylvania Court House. Meanwhile Lee called Moxley Sorrel to a sunrise meeting "under a neighboring tree" concerning who should replace the injured Longstreet as commander of I Corps. He suggested three possibilities: Major Generals Jubal A. Early, Edward Johnson, and Richard H. Anderson.

Sorrel responded candidly. Early would be unpopular because of "his flings and irritable disposition." And whereas Sorrel knew that Ed Johnson was a good friend of Lee's, Sorrel believed Johnson handicapped by the fact that he was "quite unknown to the corps." Clearly Sorrel preferred Anderson; "We *know him* and shall be satisfied with him." Sorrel left the conference convinced that Lee would select Early, no matter what objections others might raise; instead, Lee appointed Anderson.[3]

Lee did not yet understand Grant as he had McClellan, Burnside, and Hooker, who had always retired to lick their wounds after a sound whipping; nor did he comprehend that "the night of May 6 was indeed the curtain of a world drama—the struggle between opposites in life." [4] Borrowing an image from Swinton, Fuller likened Grant to Blücher, whose nickname of "Marshal Vorwarts" became on Yankee tongues "Marshal Forwarts." Blücher, in destroying Napoleon, "would hear of nothing but marching straight on Paris," and regardless of "whatever seas of blood" Grant might have to plod through, he intended to use Richmond in the same manner to destroy Lee.[5]

No one surpassed Grant in calling the Wilderness the most "desperate fighting" this continent ever had witnessed, and he admitted his losses were "very severe": 2,446 killed, 12,037 wounded, and 3,383 missing or captured (in contrast, Confederate casualties were approximated at 7,600). Yet Grant claimed a victory in having crossed the river which had divided his army from Lee's.[6]

Spotsylvania, toward which both armies now moved, has been compared to Gettysburg insofar as all roads meet there.[7] If Grant could beat Lee to this country town he would be between Richmond and the Army of Northern Virginia, thus forcing Lee to do what he least wished—attack rather than defend.

Grant was quite unprepared for the reception he received when Union troops realized that their general in chief moved "with his horse's head turned toward Richmond." Soldiers, "weary and sleepy" and "with stiffened limbs and smarting wounds," rose joyfully as they pushed to the edges of the road. Wild cheers were intermingled with cries of "On to Richmond!" Hats sailed skyward. Soldiers pushed forward, clapping their hands and speaking to Grant in a spirit of informal camaraderie. "Pine-knots and leaves were set on fire," Horace Porter recalled, "and lighted the scene with their weird, flickering glare." Even Grant's large bay horse, Cincinnati, descended from the finest racing stock in America, grew restless under the impact of the ovation. "This is most unfortunate," Grant muttered, and in order that Lee would not be awakened to the movement, staff orders were dispatched among the troops to silence their tumult.[8]

The direct route to Spotsylvania was over the Brock Road by way of Todd's Tavern, and Warren's V Corps was ordered to march this route with all possible haste and seize Spotsylvania Court House. Hancock's II Corps was to follow the same route as far as Todd's Tavern. Sedgwick's VI Corps was sent to Chancellorsville, then by way of Piney Branch Church to the Brock Road north of the Block House (so named because it was constructed of logs), and Burnside's IX Corps was expected to follow Sedgwick.

Lee had to consider the possibility that Grant could be moving toward Fredericksburg with the object of falling on the left flank of the Army of Northern Virginia. However, Anderson was told to lead Longstreet's old corps to Spotsylvania next morning. With the woods on fire, Anderson could find no safe place to bivouac and so moved off on the night of May 6 at about ten o'clock.

Now arose the mix-up between cavalry and infantry that shattered good relations between Sheridan and Meade. Little Phil sent the horse soldiers under John Irvin Gregg to hold the crossing over the Po at Snell's Bridge and the brigade under Wesley Merritt to guard the same stream at the Block House.

The cavalry under James H. Wilson was sent to take Spotsylvania, and on the morning of May 8 he reported that he had driven the enemy's cavalry through the village and was "fighting now with a considerable force." Meanwhile Meade peremptorily modified Sheridan's orders, directing Gregg to hold up at Corbin's Bridge and Merritt to advance in front of the infantry column moving down the Spotsylvania Road. It was here that, in the darkness, horse soldiers and infantrymen intermingled and delay was the reward of such confusion.

When Sheridan learned of Meade's action, Little Phil's quick temper fulfilled its reputation. Long years afterward he was still seething. "Had Gregg and Merritt been permitted to proceed as they were originally instructed, it is doubtful whether the battles fought at Spottsylvania would have occurred, for these two divisions would have encountered the enemy [Anderson] at the Po River, and so delayed his march as to enable our infantry to reach Spottsylvania first, and thus force Lee to take up a line behind the Po." In Sheridan's judgment, Meade's "disjointed and irregular orders" rendered three divisions of cavalry "practically ineffective." Warren accused Merritt of obstructing his infantry column, and Sheridan ordered Merritt off the road.

Meade called Sheridan to his headquarters where, Little Phil declared, Meade's "peppery temper had got the better of his good judgment." One heated remonstrance followed another until an exasperated Sheridan blurted that he could "whip" Jeb Stuart if Meade would only let him. When Meade reached this point in repeating the interview, Grant offered an interpolation: "Did he say so? Then let him go out and do it." [9]

Through his chief of staff, Humphreys, at one o'clock on the afternoon of May 8, Meade directed Sheridan to "proceed against the enemy's cavalry, and when your supplies are exhausted, proceed *via* New Market and Green Bay to Haxall's Landing on the James River, there communicating with General Butler, procuring supplies and return to this army. . . ."

Sheridan, receiving this order, happily took his three divisions to Aldrich's "to prepare for the contemplated expedition." To Gregg, Merritt, and Wilson, he said, "We are going out to fight Stuart's cavalry in consequence of a suggestion from me; we will give him a fair, square fight; we are strong, and I know we can beat him, and in view of my recent representations to General Meade I shall expect nothing but success." [10]

James Ewell Brown Stuart graduated from West Point in 1854. Not since the death of Thomas "Stonewall" Jackson, in '63 at Chancellorsville in this same Wilderness, was anyone more beloved in the South than Stuart, whom everyone called "Jeb." To an admiring follower, Jeb's career was "rather a page from romance than a chapter of history." The great cavalry leader of the South possessed "a flavour of chivalry and adventure which made him more like a knight of the middle ages than a soldier of the prosaic nineteenth century." War to Jeb was more poetry than science.[11]

Sheridan, "scarcely taller than a musket," [12] was not overimpressed by Stuart. Early in the morning of May 9 he put his horse soldiers on half rations and by five o'clock, with Merritt in the lead, reached Tabernacle Church and took the north-south road from Fredericksburg to Richmond. Confederate pickets spotted them passing Massaponoc Church. Their columns, between 12,000 and 15,000 troopers including artillery and wagons, stretched from eight to over thirteen miles along the road, depending on the source.[13] At any rate, they crossed three rivers that would have made a good defense for Jeb Stuart—the Ny, Po, and Ta—and neared the village of Jarrald's Mill. Sheridan, having passed this "excellent defensive line to the enemy," knew that he had gone around Lee's army "and our ability to cross the North Anna [was] placed beyond doubt." Richmond then would be "within his grasp." [14]

But Stuart, like Sheridan, was perceptive. He rode hard with the brigades of Fitzhugh "Rooney," Lee's second son, Lunsford Lomax (a classmate of Fitz Lee at West Point), and James B.

Gordon, who led the North Carolina Cavalry. On May 9, when Stuart approached the Telegraph Road from Fredericksburg to Richmond as darkness came on, it is unlikely that he had more than 4,000 men with him. Stuart wanted to reach and unite his whole command at Beaver Dam Station next day, and also hoped to see his wife Flora and their children, who were staying there at a plantation owned by Colonel Edmund Fontaine.[15]

As darkness approached and Stuart neared Telegraph Road, he learned that Sheridan had branched southwest from the main road and was aiming for Beaver Dam Station by way of Mitchell's and Chilesburg. Stuart pressed tenaciously after Sheridan's horsemen, for he knew that, in addition to his family, Beaver Dam Station contained a large part of Lee's remaining store of food and medicine. Meanwhile the Federals jogged on, cursing "the first weeks of the long drought of this famous battle summer." Men choked in the rising clouds of dust, and any halt for water or rest became a "delightful relief." Stuart sent about 1,000 men under Virginia's General Williams Wickham and Lomax to strike the rear of the Union column.

Henry R. Pyne, chaplain of the 1st New Jersey Cavalry, was part of that rear force struck by Wickham and Lomax. Confederate skirmishers and Federal flankers exchanged "flying shots," but, Pyne recalled, "every road was so well picketed along the route that it was impossible to harass or disorder our march." As the sunset began to color the sky, Pyne could see "an immense cloud of smoke" where the brigades in Sheridan's front were watering their animals in the North Anna, some eight miles or more ahead. In Pyne's regiment not a horse was turned around in the direction whence a Southern attack must come. Vedettes, or mounted sentinels, were not posted.

Lomax saw his chance and, "with a yell," charged down upon the overtrusting Federals. All hell broke loose as a brigade was driven in upon its pack train. The Union troops, Pyne said, were so completely disordered that "a disastrous panic" threatened. Unaware that the Pennsylvanians ahead of the New Jerseymen had been turned into a proper line, the Rebels swept along the road, believing they had caused a rout. "Blinded by the dust and their own eagerness," they dashed between the intervals of the Pennsylvanians. A volley pulled the Confederates up fast. The fight turned into a hand-to-hand grappling for weapons and a face-to-face exchange of blasphemous oaths. Finally the engagement could be called a stalemate: "A man or two killed, a few men wounded, an equal number of prisoners for each side, and considerable temporary confusion were all the results from an affair which threatened at first to be disastrous."

It was "very dark" when the 1st New Jersey and 1st Massachusetts barricaded the road. Occasional shots were exchanged between skirmishers—"enough to let them know we were still in position." Soldiers with axes felled trees to make the road impassable; a bridge over a nearby stream was destroyed. "Owing to the darkness and confusion," Pyne remembered, "it was midnight before we got into camp, and even then half the regiment was forced to go on picket." [16]

The Federals raised another kind of hell at Beaver Dam Station on May 9, where George A. Custer, detached from Merritt's brigade, led the raid. Custer, West Point '61, would become the following April at the age of twenty-five the youngest major general in the Union army. He rode into Beaver Dam Station after crossing the North Anna northeast of Anderson's Ford. Giving his men all the captured food and supplies they could carry, he "ordered the remainder to be burnt."

"About 1,000,000 rations of bacon and more than 500,000 of bread" were destroyed. That night the yellow clouds betokened the destruction of "flour, sugar, meal, molasses, liquor, medical stores, small arms, hospital tents." Ten miles of the tracks of the Virginia Central Railroad were torn up. One hundred cars and two locomotives were wrecked. Four hundred Union prisoners, taken in the Wilderness, were freed, cause for a "hilarious reunion." [17]

Chaplain Pyne, passing on May 10 "the smoking ruins" of Beaver Dam Station, found "some of our mechanics were still at work with axes, wrenches and sledges, to complete" the ruin of the locomotives and trains. He rejoiced in the liberation of the four hundred Yankee prisoners and added, "An immense pile of crackers and other provisions, containing two million rations, were smoldering away, and for several miles the railroad was rendered useless." [18]

Jeb Stuart's family was left unharmed.

From Beaver Dam, where Stuart later united his troops, Sheridan and his forces rode "leisurely" along the Negro Foot Road toward Richmond while Stuart was "urging his horses to the death in order to get in between Richmond and my [Sheridan's] column." This change in Jeb's tactics, Sheridan declared, left the Yankees "practically unmolested" all through May 10, and that evening they camped on the south bank of the South Anna near Ground Squirrel Bridge.[19]

But Stuart gained his objective next morning when he rode into Yellow Tavern. The place took its name from an abandoned inn whose paint had scaled as an aging man loses his hair. Within Richmond, some six miles away, frayed nerves were commonplace. Colonel Josiah Gorgas, ordnance chief, could not sleep because of "the ringing of alarm bells and the blowing of alarm whistles the most of the night." And Mrs. Alexander Lawton, whose husband was quartermaster general, remembered, "Many ladies sat up all night, dressed in their best clothes with their jewelry on." [20]

Sheridan awakened on the banks of the river that May 11. Although it was not too far into the new day, Little Phil felt greatly refreshed from his sleep and happy to procure abundant forage for his horses. By two in the morning one of Sheridan's brigades had ridden into Ashland, driven off a small body of Confederate defenders, destroyed a locomotive and a train of cars, and torn up the tracks of the Fredericksburg Railroad. These raiders rejoined Sheridan's main column at Allen's Station on the Fredericksburg & Richmond Railroad. The way to Yellow Tavern lay straight ahead.[21]

By forced marches Stuart was first to reach the country of rolling green fields and cultivated farms surrounding the abandoned inn. The day before, Major Reid Venable, a staff aide, heard Jeb mutter that "he never expected to live through the war, and that if we were to be conquered, he did not want to live." He had brought a relatively small force to Yellow Tavern, and he wired Bragg in Richmond, "My men and horses are all tired, hungry and jaded, but all right." A macadamized road led to Richmond. To a major who believed Sheridan was "too fast and too big" to catch, Jeb snorted:

"No! I would rather die than let him go!"

In Sheridan's opinion, it was the early morning raid on Ashland, through which Stuart also passed, which misled the Confederate cavalry leader, making him "so uncertain . . . that he committed the same fault that he did the first day, when he divided his force and sent a part to follow me on the Childsburg [Chilesburg] road." Again Stuart split his forces, sending a portion to fall upon Sheridan's rear while bringing the remainder—perhaps no more than 1,100 troops—to Yellow Tavern.

Sheridan believed that he could attack with almost his entire corps on May 11. He took the time—somewhere between two or three hours—to prepare carefully for the assault before he eliminated Yellow Tavern as "an uncomfortably hot place." Custer was to lead the mounted charge with General George H. Chapman on his flank and the remainder of General Wilson's division supporting him. Sheridan wrote enthusiastically:

Beginning at a walk, he [Custer] increased his gait to a trot, and then at full speed rushed the enemy. At the same moment the dismounted troops along my whole front moved forward, and as Custer went through the battery, capturing two of the guns with their cannoneers and breaking up the enemy's left, [General Alfred] Gibbs and [General Thomas C.] Devin drove his centre and right from the field.[22]

The battle was not won as handily as Sheridan suggested. To one North Carolinian it was "the most desperate hand-to-hand conflict I ever witnessed." For a time the tough 1st Maine seemed on the verge of being driven from the field, but was saved by a second mounted line and an artillery battery in the woods at Ground Squirrel Church. Thereafter sabers were freely swung.

Yet everything was wrong for the Confederates unless a miracle occurred. Ten guns, some borrowed from the Baltimore Light Artillery, were a poor match for Sheridan's estimated thirty-six guns. The charges of the Yankees continued, and one old man huddled behind a tree with a young Virginian muttered, "You do what you choose. I'm going to surrender." Still, Stuart rallied his soldiers to fight. Close to the front lines, he cried, "Boys, don't stop to count fours. Shoot them! Shoot them!"

"And we did shoot them," added a Rebel private.

But the moment was close when John A. Huff, a sharpshooter with the 5th Michigan, drew a bead on Stuart. Jeb pressed a hand to his side, his head dropped, and his hat fell off. As Jeb rested against a tree, the papers were removed from his inside pockets lest they fall into the hands of the Federals. Finally, an ambulance carried him from the field.[23]

Within twenty-four hours "the model of Virginian cavaliers" was dead. The *Richmond Examiner* squeezed every tear it could from this Confederate tragedy. One scene related a fifteen-minute visit of Jefferson Davis to "the dying chamber of his favorite chieftain."

The President, taking Stuart's hand, asked, "General, how do you feel?"

"Easy, but willing to die," Jeb replied, "if God and my country think I have fulfilled my destiny and done my duty."

No Southern heart could resist this illustration of Stuart's innate chivalry:

To Mrs. General R. E. Lee he directed that his golden spurs be given as a dying memento of his love and esteem of her husband. To his staff officers he gave his horses. So particular was he in small things, even in the dying hour, that he emphatically exhibited and illustrated the ruling passion strong in death. To one of his staff, who was a heavy-built man, he said, "You had better take the larger horse; he will carry you better." Other mementoes he disposed of in a similar manner. To his young son he left his glorious sword.

In the last moments Stuart asked the ministers around him to sing the hymn, "Rock of Ages," to which he added

all the voice his strength would permit. He then joined in prayer with the ministers. To the Doctor he again said, "I am going fast now; I am resigned; God's will be done." Thus died General J. E. B. Stuart.[24]

Beyond the deaths of Generals Stuart and James B. Gordon (who died in Richmond five days later), Yellow Tavern was a Pyrrhic victory for the North. Chaplain Pyne of the 1st New Jersey Cavalry, once across the Chickahominy, realized this fact.

In our front [he wrote, after riding around several deserted earthworks and finding the best roads into the suburbs of the Confederate capital], the road had been thickly planted with torpedoes, which the rebel prisoners, very reluctantly, were employed in taking up; their timid groping and shrinking being a curious and rather entertaining sight. . . . The impregnable fortifications of Richmond frowned along our right; the bridge over the Chickahominy had been destroyed in front; and the two provisional brigades of Richmond militia were thrown upon our rear to harass it. Beyond the Chickahominy, to defy us should we attempt to force a passage, was [the remainder of] Stuart's entire disposable cavalry; and President Davis himself had been invited to come out to witness our destruction.

Since "to ride into Richmond would have cost half the command, and the ride out have sacrificed the rest," discretion became the better part of valor. Pyne and his comrades rode on to join Butler's Army of the James.[25]

VI

★ ━━━━━━━━━━━━━━━━━━━━━━

The Bloody Angle

When Lincoln truly realized the cost of the first two days of fighting in the Wilderness, he may have been the most depressed person in the North. Congressman Schuyler Colfax of Indiana visited the White House on May 8. The legislator described Lincoln as pacing "up and down the Executive Chamber." An hour afterward, Colfax watched Lincoln receiving congressional visitors "and telling story after story to hide his saddened heart."

Next day the President was "highly pleased by the dispatches reporting the advances of Gen. Grant." At a Cabinet meeting on May 10 an obviously cheered Lincoln read the "dispatches from Gens. Grant, Butler, Sherman and others." Yet underneath the President realized that he could be relying on misleading dispatches, and on May 11 Secretary of the Navy Welles, visiting the War Department, found Lincoln anxiously waiting for news from the battle fronts.[1]

In Virginia during these same days Grant had to deal with harsh realities. Spotsylvania Court House, a pivot around which the two armies would fight for many days, stood on a ridge between two rivers, the Mattaponi and the Po. On the morning of May 9, to Grant's annoyance, the Confederates were entrenched across the Federal lines of advance. Lee's position occupied a semicircle facing north-northwest and enveloping Spotsylvania. Anderson's line on his left extended to the Po, a deep, heavily wooded, and marshy stream dangerous to cross except where bridged; General Richard S. Ewell's corps in the center occupied what was first called the "mule shoe" and later became enshrined in American history as the "Bloody Angle"; and flanking it was the corps under Early, who had replaced a still ailing General A. P. Hill.

Grant's disposition of troops placed Warren on the right where his divisions covered the Brock and other roads leading into Spotsylvania; Sedgwick was to Warren's left and Burnside's IX Corps on the extreme left. The 4th division of Hancock's corps, Mott commanding, halted at Todd's Tavern, while the remainder of Hancock's men were placed to the left of Sedgwick, between the VI Corps and Burnside. That afternoon a rebel sharpshooter killed Sedgwick, and the command of the VI Corps passed to General Horatio G. Wright, a West Point instructor who served throughout the war. Hancock by nightfall was across the left flank of Lee's army but separated from it (and the remainder of Meade's army) by the Po. Lee weakened many parts of his line to strengthen his defense against Hancock. Grant saw his advantage and ordered an afternoon attack on May 10 against Lee's center.[2]

General Gershom Mott's division was roundly scored for the laxity with which it probed Confederate pickets. In a letter home even McAllister of the 11th New Jersey admitted "we were repulsed when we ought to have been successful." Reputedly Charles Dana growled that the whole army "would have been stronger without Mott's division," adding, "They advanced into the woods with orders to attack, but came out again, like cowards." (These words are suspect since Dana's notes were ghost-written into a book by Ida M. Tarbell, and by this point in the narrative the relations between the collaborators had so deteriorated that Dana probably would not even check the proofs.)

Certainly McAllister felt no shame when he wrote his family next day:

This campaign beats all the rest in desperation and determination. God only knows the result. I expect soon to go forward again into the raging storm of lead and iron. I wrote you yesterday that I lost both my horses in battle. I had to charge through a thick woods and went on foot. We have already fought many battles; and from present appearances will have to fight many more before we get through. We are not now with the 2nd Corps. Since yesterday morning [May 10] we have been fighting with the 6th. . . .[3]

On May 9, while Stuart marched toward battle and a mortal wound two days later at Yellow Tavern, Grant received an ominous message from General Ambrose E. Burnside, who had at least two claims to fame—he had piled up the Union dead in three futile charges against an entrenched Confederate cannonade on Marye's Heights at Fredericksburg (1862) and had given his name to a style of whiskers. Dug in on the Spotsylvania–Fredericksburg road, an entirely mistaken Burnside told Grant that Lee intended to move toward Fredericksburg.

A puzzled Grant asked General Winfield Scott Hancock, who started each day with a clean shirt (from what source no one ever discovered), to cross the Po River with three divisions and, if necessary, to threaten Lee's left flank. Tall and handsome, yet with massive features that placed heavy folds under his eyes, Hancock reported early success, but the day was actually a failure and so was May 10.

Grant plunged toward the Block House Bridge on a direct road to Spotsylvania. Each probe he made on right, left, and center revealed how neatly Lee had enveloped the Federals. The division of "Little Billy" Mahone, who had risen from mailboy to railroad president, already held Block House Bridge. General Henry Heth, trained by fighting Indians in the West, swung southward by the Old Court House to strike Hancock's exposed right flank. Heth assaulted and was forced back, largely because

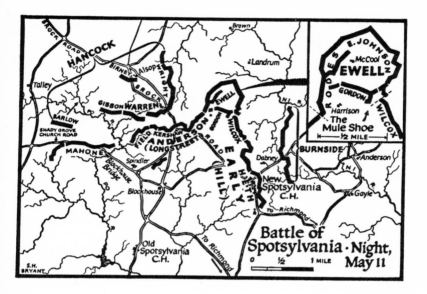

Mahone was temporarily engaged in dealing with a reconnoitering brigade on his left. Grant guessed Lee's lines must be stretched thin, ordered his V and VI Corps to attack on May 11, and paid heavily for this misjudgment.

Rain that night chilled everyone to the bone. Hancock was told to mass his II Corps for an assault on what was called Ewell's "mule shoe" salient. Twenty thousand Federals were assembled to begin the attack on May 12 at 4:30 A.M. They poured through whatever gaps they could make in the Confederate lines, fought bitterly for three-quarters of an hour, but then were halted by a second line of incomplete entrenchments. Hancock's men were happy to withdraw, for they were exhausted from slithering in the mud. New Jersey's McAllister complained that when "guns would become foul . . . we would order the men back to wash them out and return to fight on." He described the mud as "impassable." [4] At least Hancock did not return empty-handed

—his prisoners were estimated between 2,000 and 4,000. He also captured twenty cannon.[5]

Visitors to Spotsylvania, seeing the remnants of the entrenchments and rail fences where the fighting for the Bloody Angle occurred, easily accept the opinion of Horace Porter, one of Grant's aides, that the conflict was "the most desperate engagement in the history of modern warfare." Soggy leaves churned with the mud as the heavy guns were dragged forward. The breastworks were so close the opposing flags "were in places thrust against each other, and muskets were fired with muzzle against muzzle."

Whether this was "modern" or "Indian" warfare was difficult to say in this forested countryside. Rank after rank, North and South, dropped, "riddled by shot and shell and bayonet-thrusts." Fresh troops rushed forward over the masses of torn and mutilated corpses. Guns roared with double charges of canister. Fence rails and logs were splintered into dagger-size pieces that could impale a man. Madness seized the combatants, and, Porter recalled, "we not only shot down an army, but also a forest." [6]

New Jersey's McAllister, writing to Warren, his commanding general, placed the contest on intimate terms:

When the first line reached the open field at the top of the hill, in sight of the Rebel works, we rolled out a tremendous cheer. It was taken up by the second line, and our boys started forward at a run. The first line parted in the front, leaving a long open space. . . .

Here McAllister's brigade struck the salient, facing a field battery of from eight to ten guns. McAllister ordered the guns pulled back to his own works. At best he came off with eight guns. On the right he nearly carried the salient, in a contest of "life or death." McAllister saw his

massed columns pressed forward to the Salient. The Stars and Stripes and the Stars and Bars nearly touched each other across these works . . . The graycoats and bluecoats would spring with rifles in hand

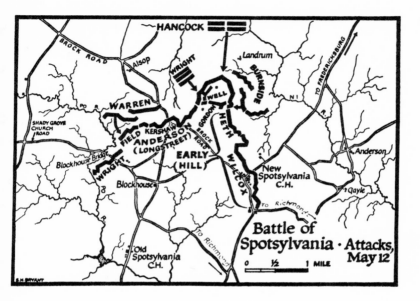

Battle of Spotsylvania · Attacks, May 12

on top of the breastworks, take deadly aim, fire, and then fall across into the trenches below. This I saw repeated again and again. . . .

The fighting lasted all day, and the rain poured down. Many of our men sunk down exhausted in the mud. Ammunition would give out, and more would be brought up. . . . It was before our line that the big tree was cut down by rifle balls [an oak tree, twenty-two inches in diameter, whose fall injured several soldiers in the 1st South Carolina Regiment]. The stump of it was exhibited [1876] at the Centennial in Philadelphia.[7]

What could not be exhibited in Philadelphia was how skulls were crushed by musket butts, men stabbed to death with swords and bayonets pushed between the logs of a parapet separating friend from foe. Wild cheers, savage yells, frantic shrieks . . . all added to this hellish duel. Neither darkness nor "the pitiless storm" could end the battle till after midnight. "Our troops had been under fire for twenty hours," Porter recorded, "but they still held the position which they had so dearly purchased." [8]

At six-thirty on the evening of this bloody May 12, Grant wrote Halleck in Washington:

The battle closes, leaving between three and four thousand prisoners in our hands for the day's work, including two general officers, and over thirty pieces of artillery. The enemy are obstinate, and seem to have found the last ditch. We have lost no organizations, not even that of a company, whilst we have destroyed and captured one division ([Edward] Johnson's), one brigade ([George] Doles'), and one regiment entire from the enemy.[9]

Although almost daily Lincoln haunted the telegraph office of the War Department, the President was greatly gratified by Grant's avowal that he intended to continue the Virginia campaign "if it takes all summer." John Nicolay, one of Lincoln's two confidential secretaries, observed in a letter to the Postmaster General on May 15 that "the President is cheerful and hopeful—not unduly elated, but seeming confident." Even friends of Secretary of War Stanton were pleased by the disappearance of the "fretfulness and impatience" which had characterized Stanton's behavior in previous years. Using General John A. Dix in New York City as his liaison, the Secretary of War good-humoredly passed along to the Associated Press copies of Grant's dispatches from Virginia.

On May 17 the President prepared an order calling for the draft of 300,000 men to "increase the active and reserved force of the Army, Navy, & Marine Corps," but there was a good reason why this order was not immediately signed. Probably the most nefarious, dangerous journalistic plot ever concocted against the Lincoln Administration now occurred.[10]

There were two perpetrators of this hoax which upset Stanton's nerves about as badly as they ever had been shaken. One was rosy-faced Joseph H. Howard, Jr., an unsavory member of the "Bohemian Brigade" who once had scooped his fellow reporters by tying up the only available telegraph line by wiring his paper the genealogy of Jesus. Other acts equally bizarre finally had made Howard unemployable and had filled him with a craze to strike back at the press and at society.

Howard's collaborator in this macabre drama was Francis A. Mallison, a one-time copyist for the Associated Press. Greed made Mallison pliable in Howard's hands, and he agreed "to filch a pad of manifold paper and some envelopes" from the AP office. Howard, who had invented the story of Lincoln en route to his inauguration sneaking into Baltimore in "a Scotch cap and long military cloak," now displayed the remarkable dimensions of his imagination. In a bogus proclamation dated May 17, 1864, Howard wrote sadly of how in Virginia Grant "has crippled" the strength of the Army of the Potomac and "defeated" its plans; when Lincoln coupled to this "the disaster at Red River, the delay at Charleston, and the general state of the country," he was obliged to set May 26 "as a day of fasting, humiliation and prayer"; and, furthermore, to call for another 400,000 troops, between the ages of eighteen and forty-five, to bolster the Union's dispirited armies.

Mallison, hoping "to make a killing in the gold market, since the price of gold in terms of greenbacks was bound to soar on the adverse news," used a stylus to forge the signatures of Lincoln and Secretary of State Seward to Howard's literary fraud. At three o'clock in the morning Mallison and "a well-coached urchin" dashed along New York's Park Row, distributing copies of the story. Lorenzo L. Carounse, night clerk of the *New York Daily News*, quizzed the Associated Press to ascertain if the dispatch were correct. Back came the reply: "It is as false as hell." [11]

Only two rabidly anti-Lincoln papers in New York, the *World* and the *Journal of Commerce*, published the false proclamation. Even so, by 10:00 A.M., or before the papers denying the story's credibility appeared on the street, the price of gold rose eight points on the market.[12] A probably wild-eyed Seward dashed into the War Department. Good God, this was "steamer day," when newspapers were carried abroad; if this news reached Europe, no one could tell what harm it might do the Union!

An outraged Stanton believed he knew the culprits: the Independent Telegraph Company, a competitor of the Associated Press. Without waiting for proof, Stanton ordered the seizure of the books and the arrest of the employees of the Independent Telegraph Company, not only in Washington but also in New York, Philadelphia, Baltimore, Harrisburg, and Pittsburgh. Given a free hand, Stanton would have filled the cells of Old Capitol Prison.

Howard and Mallison were arrested also and incarcerated in Fort Lafayette. Lincoln released Howard after three months and Mallison a month later because the President had grown tired of "certain 'Democratic' stumpers," like Mallison's "aged mother," who were "making a handle of continued confinement." In brief, Lincoln possessed worries far more serious than Mallison.[13]

At Spotsylvania, after the ferocious fighting at the Bloody Angle on May 12, the heavy downpour and mud brought both armies to a virtual standstill. Through four days of rain, Lee was harried by grim reflections. The inability of the Confederates to drive Grant's men from the Bloody Angle had to be compared to the disaster of Pickett's Charge at Gettysburg (and again, to save face for his subordinates, Lee claimed the responsibility for this plight at Spotsylvania as once he had accepted full blame for defeat at Gettysburg). Ewell placed his casualties at 2,000, but the Federals raised the Confederate loss to 3,000. Lee had suffered five general officers killed or mortally injured, nine wounded and two captured.[14]

Lee, who occasionally napped on a plank raised on a rail, started his worrisome days at three o'clock in the morning. In order to divine Grant's intentions, he decided he must cover Snell's Bridge, a crossing of the Po on the way to Richmond. To achieve this objective, however, the Confederates must take a hill commanding the front lines, an assignment entrusted to the III Corps brigade under a former Georgia politician, General Ambrose R. Wright. The attack was so poorly handled that General Hill, watching from the rear of a nearby church, thundered at the blundering Wright and his needless casualties. Standing beside Hill, Lee spoke quietly.

These men are not an army. They are citizens defending their country. General Wright is not a soldier; he's a lawyer. . . . If you humiliated General Wright, the people of Georgia would not understand. Besides, whom would you put in his place? You'll have to do what I do: When a man makes a mistake, I call him to my tent, talk to him, and use the authority of my position to make him do the right thing the next time.[15]

Lee had bright moments also. On May 15, General John C. Breckinridge, assisted by a battalion of cadets from Virginia Military Institute, drove the Union forces under Franz Sigel from the upper Shenandoah Valley; on the 16th, General Pierre G. T. Beauregard struck Butler from below Drewry's Bluff and hurled the Army of the James back to Bermuda Hundred Neck whence, for any possible usefulness in attacking Richmond, he was (to use Grant's disgusted phrase) "in a bottle strongly corked."

Probes and skirmishes convinced Lee that Grant was preparing to move again. Few of the reinforcements Lee so desperately needed could be promised, whereas Washington sent Grant a brigade of 2,000 from the Irish Regiment and 7,500 heavy artillerymen retrained to fight as the 4th Division of the II Corps. On May 19 Grant was again "sidling to the left" or edging nearer Richmond with Lee in dogged pursuit. Well could Grant seek another field of action—Spotsylvania probably had cost him 17,000 casualties against 12,000 for Lee. Colonel Theodore Lyman marveled at the morale of the Southern people as the Wilderness campaign entered its third phase:

I have just seen a man of 48 [Lyman wrote], very much crippled with rheumatism, who said he was enrolled two days ago. He told them [the Confederates] he had thirteen persons dependent on him, including three grandchildren (his son-in-law had been taken some time since); but they said that made no difference; he was on his way to the rendezvous, when our cavalry crossed the river, and he hid in the bushes, till they came up. I offered him money for some of his small vegetables; but he said: "If you have any bread, I would rather have it. Your cavalry have taken all the corn I had left, and, as for meat, I have not tasted a mouthful for six weeks." If you had seen his eyes glisten when I gave him a piece of salt pork, you would have believed his story. He looked like a man who had come into a fortune. "Why," said he, "that must weigh four pounds—that would cost me forty dollars in Richmond! They told us they would feed the families of those that were taken; and so they did for two months, and then they said they had no more meal." [16]

The next invaders of the Wilderness would be the trumpet vine and the honeysuckle.

VII

The Spreading
Web of War

Traveling southward from Spotsylvania, Robert Mc-Allister brooded over what the fighting in the Wilderness had cost him. In addition to the two horses shot during these battles, there were other personal losses for which the Federal government should compensate his family if he failed to survive the Virginia campaign. A man who methodically wound his watch at the same hour every evening, McAllister listed these items for his wife, Ellen:

Black horse	$300
Charley	200
navy revolvers	75
equipments	25
	$600

There was a chance, McAllister admitted, that the government might not pay more for the black horse; but then, as he later confessed to his daughter Hennie, he could be prejudiced in favor of Charley, who had served him in the battle against Longstreet for the plank road (May 6):

I then mounted Charley. The enemy soon made an attack. It was a furious one. It was massed troops trying to make the attack so as to break our center. Charley never seemed to be more in his element than he was in this battle. I rode the lines back and forward. He carried his head amidst the roar of cannon and musketry and entered into the very spirit of the contest. Near the close a ball passed through his neck through the large arteries. The blood pressed out on both sides of his neck in large streams. I dismounted; and just as I reached the ground, another ball hit him in the shoulder. He jumped back, pulled the reins out of my hand, and went off at a gallop with the blood streaming from him. I never saw him again, but heard of him lying dead a short distance from the scene of action.[1]

In the end, a military campaign became a strange mixture of personal recollections.

Although the movement was somewhat slow, the cleanness with which the Army of Northern Virginia disengaged itself from Spotsylvania pleased Lee. The paucity of straggling was more remarkable considering the fact that only the least experienced of his corps commanders, Anderson, appeared fit for duty. A. P. Hill still wobbled from his recent illness, and Ewell verged on imminent collapse. Lee had sound cause for choosing as his next line of defense the deep bank of the North Anna, twenty-three miles north of Richmond, since the river provided a natural barrier to a direct Federal frontal assault. If, however, Grant aimed at the Confederate capital from the northeast by way of the Mattaponi, Lee could without undue effort shift his Southern divisions to the Pamunkey.[2]

Grant also was happy "sideslipping" Spotsylvania. The roads were good, the country well cultivated, although "No men were seen except those bearing arms, even the black man having been sent away." For Grant, in a strange region without guides or adequate maps, this circumstance posed a real handicap. At least he relieved the burden of the march by returning to Washington more than a hundred pieces of artillery, with horses and caissons, which he believed could not be "advantageously used."

Hancock led the march easterly along the Fredericksburg Railroad to Guiney's Station, then southerly to Bowling Green and

Milford on May 21. Here Hancock met a detachment of General George E. Pickett's division, en route from Richmond to reinforce Lee, but Grant brushed aside the subsequent skirmish: "They were speedily driven away, and several hundred captured." Warren, following Hancock, reached Guiney's Station that night "without molestation." Burnside and Wright remained at Spotsylvania "to keep up the appearance of an intended assault" and so hold Lee while Hancock and Warren were interposed between the Army of Northern Virginia and Richmond. But Grant was fretful:

Lee had now a superb opportunity to take the initiative either by attacking Wright and Burnside alone, or by following by the Telegraph Road and striking Hancock's and Warren's corps, or even Hancock's alone, before reinforcements could come up. But he did not avail himself of either opportunity. He seemed really to be misled as to my designs; but moved by his interior line—the Telegraph Road—to make sure of keeping between his capital and the Army of the Potomac. He never again had such an opportunity of dealing a heavy blow.[3]

Had Grant thought through the situation more objectively, he would have realized that Lee at the moment was in no condition to contemplate taking the offensive.

On the 19th at Spotsylvania there was a brisk little affair called the Battle at Harris's Farm. Many of the Federals, according to McAllister, were recruits from Washington untrained in warfare, resulting in a panic that found them firing into each other with fearful loss. An artillery quartermaster probably supplied the best account of the affair: "First there was [John H.] Kitching's brigade firing at the enemy; then [Robert O.] Tyler's men fired into his; up came [William] Birney's division and fired into Tyler's; while the artillery fired at the whole damned lot." The 1st Maine Heavy Artillery lost 466 men. About 500 Confederates were captured. McAllister's old commander, General Gershom Mott, unable to stand up to the criticism of the mismanaged battle, "has killed himself"—meaning that he had lost respect.[4]

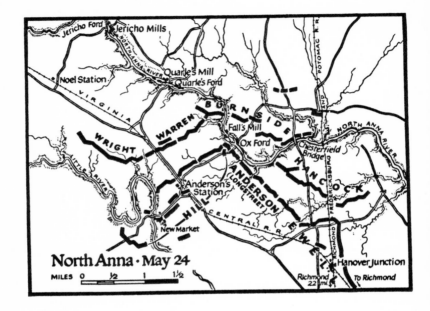

North Anna · May 24
MILES 0   ½   1   1½

On the morning of May 21 Burnside and Wright moved to join Grant's army and were at Guiney's Station next morning. Thus the parts of the force came together like pieces on a chessboard until they faced Lee at the North Anna. Here on May 23 the Federals' V Corps hit hard at the Confederate left. The blow was countered by Hill, and especially by the division under Cadmus Wilcox, who sustained 642 casualties. Lee, suffering with a severe intestinal ailment, reacted as should have been expected whenever illness cracked the hard edge of his composure. He stormed down on Hill.

"Why," Lee demanded, "did you not do as [Stonewall] Jackson would have done—thrown your whole force upon those people and driven them back?"

Wisely Hill offered no rebuttal.

With Grant astride the North Anna at Ox Ford, so that to get from one wing to the other he must twice cross the river, Lee sensed his chance to smash one wing of the Federal army.

If only Jackson had lived or Longstreet had recovered from his wounds, Lee would have trusted them with the army he was too sick to lead.

"We must strike them a blow—we must never let them pass us again—we must strike them a blow," he moaned, rolling on his cot.

And again:

"We must destroy this Army of Grant's before he gets to James River. If he gets there it will become a siege, and then it will be a mere question of time."

The one note of cheer, during these days of physical disability, was the arrival of about 8,000 reinforcements—George Pickett's division, placed with the III Corps; Robert Hoke's old brigade, returned from North Carolina; and two brigades under Breckinridge, who recently had whipped Franz Sigel in the Valley.[5]

Grant's sense of humor sometimes possessed the dry quality of a Lincoln. Thus the General could write in the *Official Records,* "Finding the enemy's position on the North Anna stronger than either of his previous ones, I withdrew on the night of the 26th." [6]

One day when Grant was sideslipping southward from the North Anna, he sat on the porch of a plantation and watched Burnside's corps passing by. Meade and his staff, who had accompanied Grant, understood why the general in chief was in a jovial mood; he recently had received official intelligence that Sherman had crossed the Etowah River and entered Georgia. To the group on the porch were added Mrs. Tyler, "the lady of the house," and an elderly woman; and presently Burnside walked up with "his big spurs and saber rattling." Burnside touched his hat politely to the ladies and observed that he suspected they never before had seen so many "live Yankees."

"Oh yes, I have," said the elderly woman. "Many more."

"Where?" Burnside asked.

"In Richmond." Clearly the elderly woman referred to Union prisoners.

Grant read aloud his official dispatch. Mrs. Tyler burst into tears. The woman, Grant reasoned, had believed Southern reports "that Lee was driving us from the State in the most demoralized condition" and now could see with her own eyes how untrue such accounts were. Mrs. Tyler dried her eyes long enough to ask if the news about Sherman was also correct. Grant answered that there could be no doubt about it. On leaving, Grant placed a guard to protect her home, and then, as if to ease his own embarrassment, added, "If your husband is hiding you can bring him in and he shall be protected also." [7]

The war was not only a game of over-all generalship between Grant and Lee but also a tale of two cities: Washington and Richmond. Lincoln could cheer Governor John Brough of Ohio by quoting Grant's comment that "everything looks exceedingly favorable to us," but a stout heart and an unwavering faith that somehow Grant would muddle through to victory were required to accept this statement.[8] Even Washington's springtime blossoms could not hide the stench of the boats bringing to the Sixth Street wharf the wounded from the first two days of fighting in the Wilderness. At night the torches of the ambulances lined up to receive them cast glittering reflections on the surface of the darkened Potomac. On May 21 the *Washington Chronicle* published a list of 18,000 who were slightly wounded and prisoners of war. At last the scaffolding was removed from the statue of Armed Freedom atop the Capitol; the cynical could find grim humor in that fact. But the true spirit of Washington in these trying hours was better captured by Margaret Leech:

Hundreds of men and women went to the wharves to deal out food and drink, and to pour water on the dressings, which had dried and stiffened on the journey. Little darkies ran beside the ambulances with drinking water. Along the route to the hospitals, people set tables in the street before their houses, and offered tea, coffee and sandwiches as the trains moved slowly past. The hospitals were surrounded with volunteer nurses and friends of the wounded. Crowds of strangers added to the turmoil of the city—anxious people hurrying through the streets, scanning the newspapers, bending over rows of stretchers and cots, each looking for one certain face, hoping and dreading to find it.[9]

As tents mushroomed on the grounds of the hospitals in and about Washington, the Sanitary Commission on F Street supplied materials like morphine, chloroform, opium, scissors, forceps, and chloride of lime which should have come from a woefully disorganized Medical Bureau. Since the railroads south were soon declared indispensable for military use, the wounded were received in a hospital at Fredericksburg and transported down Aquia Creek to Belle Plain—a "bottomless swamp" in times of heavy rain. Usually a ten-mile ride by mule-drawn ambulance awaited the sick and wounded. If the animals became stuck in the mud, the unfortunate passengers could only moan and groan while the drivers cursed and cracked their whips; but, even so, the poor devils within the ambulances may not have been worse off than in dry weather when the rough and rutted roads bounced them mercilessly. The possibility of guerrilla attack also existed, and some deaths resulted from overturned wagons.[10]

The moment was propitious for a remarkable woman, Clara Barton, to appear on the scene. Now in her early forties, Miss Barton traced her New England conscience back to 1640 when the first Barton had landed at Salem, Massachusetts. What Clara learned about hardheadedness came from growing up without childhood friends; what she learned about war came principally from the legends of a father who had fought Indians with "Mad Anthony" Wayne; and what she learned about nursing stemmed from the care she bestowed upon her brother David, who for two years suffered the pain and humiliation of an invalid.

Except for a brief period attached to the troops under Butler, Clara Barton served for four years without pay in a war where male nurses far outnumbered females. Miss Barton, wrote one authority, "was a one-man relief-agency rather than a nurse," and no one could count the number of battlefields she had visited. Hers was the kind of mind, for example, which could latch onto the fact that there were four hundred fewer ambulances in the

Wilderness than at Gettysburg. Despite the refreshment stations established by Christian Commission delegates at Belle Plain and elsewhere along the route to Fredericksburg, she was aghast at the conditions she found. Most of all her heart went out to the "walking-wounded," who were expected to make their own way on foot from Belle Plain to Washington.[11]

There was fire in Clara Barton's eyes when she stamped into the office of Senator Henry Wilson of Massachusetts (a fire that Stanton often encountered when he tried to cross her). Wilson stood not by the hour—it was ten o'clock at night—when he accompanied Miss Barton to the War Department. Their ultimatum was simple and clear: either the War Department cleaned up this mess or the Senate would. At six next morning quartermaster General Montgomery C. Meigs was inspecting the situation at the Sixth Street wharf. Private homes were opened to relieve hospital overcrowding in Fredericksburg. A railroad commenced operations between Belle Plain and Washington.[12]

Denigrating Grant became the new fad in taut and nervous Richmond. Fantasies had flourished in the Confederacy since 1861 when Lincoln, in trying to feed hungry soldiers within Fort Sumter, was charged with provoking a war. Tartness also was a Southern characteristic of speech, ranging from the accusation that Davis treated Congress like "a nose of wax in [his] fingers" to the outcry of that self-styled Napoleon and New Orleans Creole, General Pierre G. T. Beauregard, who minced no words in his dislike of the President: "The curse of God must have been on our people when we chose him." [13] Thomas Cooper DeLeon, who as a journalist, novelist, and Confederate officer lived through the war in Confederate capitals, in February categorized Grant as bringing forward "a quadruple brood of ridiculous mice" and summarized in a paragraph the general (and mistaken) Richmond view of the Union leader:

Had he embarked his troops in transports and sailed up the river, Grant might have landed his army at White House [Virginia] in twenty-four hours; and that without the firing of a shot. But he had chosen a route that was to prove him not only the greatest strategist of the age, but the most successful as well. The difference of the two was simply this: he took twenty-six days instead of one; he fought nine bloody engagements instead of none; he made four separate changes in his digested plan of advance; and he lost 70,000 men to gain a position a condemned general had occupied two years before without a skirmish! [14]

Despite the threat of Grant's advancing army, DeLeon found Richmond quiet and calm. Yet even he admitted that Lee was being supplied by "very imperfect systems." He admired extremely "the first ladies of the land," who took humble positions as clerks in arsenals or factories or at the desks of accountants and "performed their labor faithfully, earnestly and well." The Wilderness, DeLeon believed, had bolstered "waning confidence in the valor of men, and discretion of the general"; and after Spotsylvania he sneered anew at Grant's advance billing as the "greatest strategist since Napoleon." [15]

John B. Jones, a dedicated clerk in the Confederate War Department, saw Richmond in a different perspective. As early as May 12 he heard that preparations had been completed for the President and his Cabinet to escape by the Danville Road, "in the event of the fall of the city," and next day agonized over the rumor that Butler had cut this road. Later it seemed that Butler only had blown up some coal pits, causing Jones to comment that Butler's bluecoats "cannot *blow* coal *higher* than our own extortionate people have done." Telegraph wires had been cut around the city so that dispatches from Lee had to be delivered by couriers. Next day Jones heard that Grant's troops had gone into battle at Spotsylvania, "stimulated by whiskey rations." The *Examiner* twitted the "cowardice" of those members of Congress who wished to rush home. Instead of accepting the resignation of John C. Pemberton, whom Grant had defeated at Vicksburg, Davis made Pemberton lieutenant colonel of artillery. Again the President was clinging to favorites as he had with Braxton Bragg, who after his failures in Tennessee had been called to Richmond to act as Davis's chief military adviser. No two officers, Jones declared, were more "obnoxious both to the people and the army." [16]

Beauregard, who had started the war at Sumter, was now at Petersburg and sent an aide to Richmond seeking troops and permission to smash Butler, then to act as a wing to Lee's army in defeating Grant and opening the way to dictating peace terms to Lincoln. Davis pleaded illness in not receiving the aide, and Bragg listened politely. Jefferson Davis's change of heart toward Beauregard, however, concerned only assaulting Butler. Matthew W. Ransom's North Carolinians were sent to bolster Beauregard, who had added three artillery battalions to his 20,000 infantrymen; and the dapper Creole was further reinforced by James Dearing's cavalry brigade of about 1,600. A complicated pincers movement against Butler foundered when the "parts" of Beauregard's pick-up command failed to coordinate properly. Butler retained his base on May 16, but he was badly shaken. Moreover, he forgot that the end of the peninsula his river base occupied was not much more than three miles from the James River to the Appomattox. Beauregard stretched his lines between these streams, rolled up his heavy guns, and had Butler neatly caged! [17]

War Clerk Jones was exuberant over this victory and noted sourly in his diary, "Gens. Bragg and Pemberton made an inspection of the position of the enemy, down the river, yesterday [May 15], and made rather a cheerless report to the President. They are both supposed to be inimical to Gen. Beauregard, who seems to be achieving such brilliant success."

Colonel Lucius Northrop—one day he would stand trial and be acquitted on the charge of inadequately feeding Union prisoners—knew his Richmond politics well enough to call Beauregard a "charlatan." By May 22, a clear, warm, and sunny day but one when "the atmosphere is charged with the smoke and dust of contending armies," Jones faced the more personal problem that flour was selling at $400 a barrel, meal at $125 a bushel. Next day Jones heard that Grant was "worming" eastward toward the position on the Peninsula occupied by George B. McClellan in '62; as though leaning over DeLeon's shoulder and copying a sentence, Jones added, "Why, he [Grant] might have attained that position without the loss of a man at the outset!" On the 24th Jones reported ominously, "An armed guard is now a fixture before the President's house," and he was delighted on the 27th when "the *Whig* and *Enquirer* both denounced Gen. Bragg." [18]

Across the broad spectrum of the war a single day could have many meanings. On May 27, 1864, for example, in Chicago, Augustus N. Dickens, brother of the English novelist Charles Dickens, requested Lincoln's autograph as a keepsake. In Washington the President won the friendship of Congressman John F. Driggs of Michigan by shaking hands with the "gentleman and two ladies from Connecticut" brought to the White House by Driggs's son. In Richmond a dispute between Bragg and Beauregard led Jones to say, "There may be some design against the President in all this." And after "the greatest unfought repulse of the war" on the North Anna, this was the day when Grant's maneuvers "certainly looked like an attempt to turn Lee and drive on to the capital from a new angle." [19]

Lee's continuing cramps prevented him from mounting a horse on May 27. As the Army of Northern Virginia left the North Anna to cut off Grant from Richmond, Lee rode in a carriage with the II Corps. The general in chief's dullness of spirit remained after a march of fifteen miles straight south on the Telegraph Road brought the troops to an encampment near Atlee's, a station about nine miles from the Confederate capital on the Virginia Central Railroad.

"I am not fit to command this army," Lee said.[20]

Robert E. Lee, Jr., was aghast to contemplate what it would mean if his father—this man whom General Early called "the head and front, the very life and soul of the army"—were permanently disabled. "It could not be!" young Lee exclaimed. "It was too awful to consider!" [21]

But Adjutant General Walter H. Taylor, "the closest of all staff officers" to Lee, admitted that the general in chief's indisposition "was more serious than was generally supposed." Taylor was distressed over Lee's depression since Taylor believed, "Our army is in excellent condition; its *morale* as good as when we met Grant." And Taylor understood that more than physical pain upset Lee. The wounded Longstreet was still lost to him, and Ewell had been so weakened by an attack of severe diarrhea that he had to be sent off on sick leave. The greatest loss, of course, was Stuart, who had been "the eyes of the army." Lee wished he could replace Jeb with his son Rooney, but he could well imagine how the gossip about nepotism would go on behind the fluttering fans in Richmond. In the end the leader of each cavalry division was placed in an independent command. From the North Anna, in Taylor's opinion, Grant made "another detour" to the east and Lee "moved upon a parallel line."

In another three days his health had definitely improved.[22]

VIII

Should Lincoln
Be Dumped?

The emotional impact of the war on Washington—
that "vast practical joke," as one London journalist called the
capital—emphasized the breakdown in morals that inevitably ac-
companies a disruption in government. The population of prosti-
tutes in Washington was estimated at 5,000, with an overflow of
2,000 in Georgetown and Alexandria. Brothels littered such
notorious areas as Nigger Hill and Tincup Alley and were located
in respectable neighborhoods as well, with one situated only a
block from the White House. But the classic case was the
bordello adjoining the First Baptist Church on Thirteenth Street,
so that on a Sabbath the ladies proceeded to their respective
callings with noses haughtily uplifted.

Many found amusement in the groups bearing signs of "Pick-
pocket and Thief" who marched down Pennsylvania Avenue
followed by fife and drum corps playing "The Rogue's March,"
but these isolated episodes did not stop the mugging or robbery,
the brawls and the shootings. Newspapers openly described the
numerous "gambling hells" that were tailored to the tastes and
incomes of their clienteles. Women smuggled in rotgut whiskey
tied to their posteriors beneath their hoopskirts. Others employed oversized "lacteal fountains" in these clandestine visits.

For a man who must earn $1,333 a year to support a family of five, there was natural resentment toward these illicit practitioners who were pushing up the high cost of living. Strikes became commonplace and generally successful—among mechanics and laborers who wanted their half hour for lunch extended to an hour, among bookbinders at the Government Printing Office who bargained to have their ten hours a day reduced to eight hours or their weekly salaries raised from $16 to $18, among drivers of the street railways who demanded that their daily wage of $1.50 become $1.75—and at one time or another every type of employment, including the girls in the Treasury Department, was involved in similar negotiations. Even Lincoln was rebuked for spending money on the Capitol that could have been used in financing the war.

"If people see the Capitol go on," the President replied, "it is a sign we intend the Union shall go on."

Lincoln approved on April 22, 1864, a bill that placed the inscription "In God We Trust" on coins (the motto was first used on a two-cent piece). His only consistent amusement to relieve his official duties was attending the theater. Sometimes he would join one of his secretaries, John Hay, and laugh at the attacks on Jefferson Davis in the *Richmond Examiner*. But these escapes could not lighten his war-saddened heart.

Lincoln learned more than many around him ever suspected. Even before the North heard of Grant's staggering losses in the Wilderness, Lincoln surmised that there were those who considered him a political risk. Radicals muttered that he would be far too "soft" on reconstruction; conservatives believed he too hastily violated civil rights; and others bore scars, some imaginary, some real, as a result of the manner in which they had been slighted in the distribution of patronage. In Missouri and New York, local politicians believed they would run stronger with someone else heading the national ticket.

What stymied them, however, was Lincoln's popularity with

the masses of the people. Still, a group of sixteen of the most important Republicans in New York, calling themselves "friends of the Government and supporters of the present Administration," addressed Lincoln on March 25. They believed the country was not "now in position to enter into a presidential contest" and urged that Lincoln delay the national convention to the first of September or even later, if possible.[1]

Lincoln received stacks of letters, suggesting distrust of his political power. Joseph Medill's *Chicago Tribune* continued to endorse Lincoln, but in a private letter to Elihu B. Washburne of April 12 Medill believed that "Lincoln has some very weak and foolish traits of character." Unless the President "cut loose from the semi-copperheads in his Cabinet" and put "live bold vigorous radicals in their places," Medill saw no chance of electing Lincoln even if he were nominated. Dump Lincoln and who would replace him? Medill leaned toward Grant "if he continues to be successful in battlefield." [2]

Alexander K. McClure, delegate-at-large from Pennsylvania on his way to the Baltimore convention of the National Union Party on June 7, stopped by to see the President. Lincoln greeted him cordially, willing to mend political fences wherever and with whomever he could. Perhaps it was then, as McClure seems to suggest, that Lincoln explained why in place of Hannibal Hamlin of Maine the vice-presidential nomination should go to Andrew Johnson, Unionist and governor of Tennessee. In Lincoln's estimation Johnson "was the most conspicuous, most aggressive, and the most able of all the War Democrats"; and, moreover, Union sentiment would be stimulated abroad by the "election of a representative Southern man . . . from one of the rebellious states in the very heart of the Confederacy." [3]

War Democrats and Republicans met in common cause at the National Union convention in Baltimore, "welcomed by a splendid band, from Fort McHenry." Many ladies "graced" the tier of boxes. On June 8, the second day of the assemblage, B. C. Cook of Illinois gained the floor. "Mr. President," he shouted, "the State of Illinois again presents to the loyal people of this Nation, for President of the United States, Abraham Lincoln. God bless him."

William M. Stone of Iowa instantly leaped to his feet. "In the name of the Great West," his deep voice roared, "I demand that the roll be called."

Politicians who believed Lincoln could not be elected were not going to make this admission in public. The Lincoln bandwagon picked up speed as the secretary of the convention intoned the roll of the states—a performance of profound dullness except that occasionally a state added its own divertissement to the roll call. Thus Pennsylvania cast fifty-two votes "for Abraham Lincoln, 'nigger' troops, and all"; Tennessee declared that unless Lincoln were nominated, the act "would be regarded both at home and abroad as a concession of something to the Rebellion"; and Nebraska gave her six votes to "Abraham Lincoln, whom we regard as the second saviour of the world."

J. F. Hume was clearly embarrassed when the roll reached Missouri. By state instruction, he said, Missouri must cast its twenty-two votes "for the man who stands at the head of the fighting Radicals of the nation, Ulysses S. Grant." Once the tally was announced, Hume switched Missouri's vote and Lincoln's nomination became unanimous. Later that day Andrew Johnson was added to the ticket.[4]

Despite the band thumping "Hail Columbia" and "Yankee Doodle," Attorney General Edward Bates was greatly "surprised and mortified" by the convention. Lincoln's nomination, Bates believed, was managed by the delegates as though "the object were to defeat their own nomination." "They *rejected*," the Attorney General confided in his diary, "the only delegates from Mo. who were instructed and pledged for Lincoln, and admitted the *destructives*, who were *pledged against Lincoln*, and, in fact, voted against him, *falsely alleging* that they were instructed to vote for Grant!"

The President was going to receive an earful when Edward Bates returned to Washington.[5]

Earlier, sheer vanity and ambition had led the Secretary of the Treasury, Ohio's Salmon P. Chase, to contemplate wresting the presidential nomination from Lincoln. The rumor mills in Washington whirred with stories of how the secretary was employing 10,000 treasury agents to organize Chase-for-President clubs throughout the country. Postmaster General Montgomery C. Blair so thoroughly disliked Chase he would accept any tale of how the Ohioan "would cut the President's throat" at the first opportunity; but the legalistic mind of Attorney General Bates was more moderate even if Chase had been particularly lax in attending recent Cabinet meetings. Secretary of War Stanton, professing intense bitterness toward Chase, still had asked the Ohioan to be godfather at the baptism of his granddaughter. Outwardly Stanton appeared unwavering in his loyalty to Lincoln, yet nobody could be sure of where, unseen, a love for intrigue might carry him.

Soon Washington brought a new twist to the Chase story, involving Senator Samuel C. Pomeroy of Kansas, who was Chase's campaign manager by self-appointment. Pomeroy circulated a letter that eulogized Chase and severely rebuked the President. A stunned Chase, resignation in hand, rushed to the Executive Mansion. He had neither authorized nor known the contents of the letter. Lincoln smilingly gave Chase the benefit of the doubt and refused his resignation. Ohio Republicans supported Lincoln solidly in their preconvention balloting, and Chase's presidential hopes died when he could not carry his own state. Behind the scenes Stanton and Secretary of State Seward chuckled as if Chase's embarrassment was the year's greatest joke.[6]

Reconstruction was the hard core of dissension between Lincoln and the extreme Republican Radicals. Lincoln took the view that constitutionally the Southern states could not secede and so maintained that he was dealing with rebellious individuals and not political bodies. Southern prisoners—"galvanized Yankees"—who admitted the error of their ways and took an oath of allegiance to the Union satisfied the President. By his reasoning, any state with 10 per cent of its voters in 1860 accepting the Federal position on slavery and taking oaths of allegiance should be welcomed back into the Union. Working for weeks with the War Department, four Southern states partially controlled by the Union —Louisiana, Arkansas, Tennessee, and Virginia—were judged ready for readmission. Virginia was a test case. A Unionist minority from Alexandria, led by Francis H. Pierpont, marched up Capitol Hill, hats in hand. Congress refused to receive them. Without support of the Union army this delegation never would have existed, a fact that Lincoln could not deny.

At the moment two senators, Benjamin F. Wade of Ohio and Henry W. Davis of Maryland, were discussing the kind of bill that would be necessary for a workable reconstruction. Lincoln doubtless would veto the bill, but then Lincoln could be damned; Congress and not the President controlled the readmission of the states. The Wade-Davis bill, which was not passed or vetoed until July, foretold why reconstruction produced stormy times. By the Wade-Davis formula, provisional governors would take over the Southern states until the war ended; civil government would be restored when half the white male population took the oath of loyalty; no Confederate officers or volunteer soldiers could hold state office; slavery must be forever abolished; Confederate debts were to be repudiated; and state constitutions must be amended to bar ex-Confederates from any position of power.

Meanwhile, on May 31, a group calling itself the "Radical Men of the Nation" and composed of about equal numbers of extreme Radical Republicans, German liberals and Eastern abolitionists, convened in Cleveland's Cosmopolitan Hall to oppose, in the words of the *Chicago Times*, those "wire-pullers and bottle-washers" who backed Lincoln. (Along with such prominent figures as Elizabeth Cady Stanton were others bearing the incredible names of Caspar Butz and Pantaleon Candidus.)

Planks in the platform of this splinter party ranged from the constitutional prohibition of slavery to a one-term presidency. The fire-eating abolitionist from Boston, Wendell Phillips, unable to be in Cleveland, sent a letter that rang with phrases of Republican revolt:

We have three tools with which to crush the rebellion—men, money, and the emancipation of the negro. . . . For three years the [Lincoln] Administration has lavished money without stint, and drenched the land in blood, and it has not yet thoroughly and heartily struck at the slave system. . . . Mr. Lincoln may wish the end—peace and freedom —but he is wholly unwilling to use the means which can secure that end. . . .[7]

In place of Lincoln, Mr. Phillips said, "we shall fling our candidate's name, the long-honored one of J[ohn] C. Frémont, to the breeze"—far more honored for his explorations than for his generalship, Mr. Phillips could have added. For a running mate to Frémont, the Cleveland convention selected a superpolitician, the Honorable John Cochrane, Attorney General of New York, who had "thrown an anchor to windward by visiting Mr. Lincoln before the Convention met and assuring him of his continued friendship."

The Cleveland affair highly amused Lincoln. Told that about four hundred delegates had attended, the President reached "for the Bible which commonly lay on his desk" and read to his two secretaries, " 'And every one that was in distress, and every one that was in debt, and every one that was discontented, gathered themselves unto him; and he became a captain over them: and there was with him about four hundred men.' " [8]

The height of absurdity produced by the rumor mills in Washington was the suggestion that Lincoln be replaced on the ballot by General Benjamin F. Butler, who during his military occupancy of New Orleans had won the unenviable nickname of "Beast." The scheme, however, "failed to catch fire." [9] But the professional politicians bordered on panic and each night prayed that some military achievement would brighten the Republican prospects. Later Frémont and Cochrane withdrew from the election so that Lincoln would have the "full" support of the Republican Party.

IX

The Great Battle Impends

Although the Republicans neared hysteria, Grant's mood was highly optimistic when he left the North Anna late in May. "Lee's army is really whipped," he wired Washington, and in one sense it was, for Grant no longer believed that wherever Lee went Meade should follow. Now Grant's plan was much "bolder," insisting that wherever *Meade* went *Lee* should be compelled to follow. But another part of Grant's strategy—to force Lee to fight in the open—had failed tactically, and, he freely admitted to Washington, he could no longer expect "a battle with [Lee] outside of intrenchments." [1]

Grant ordered his base of supplies to the Virginia village of White House on the Pamunkey, and through prior arrangement with Halleck in the War Department the Navy was to move supplies by water. Also, previous instructions to Butler, in command of the Army of the James, asked that Baldy Smith's corps of about 16,000 be shifted to guard the base at White House. In a letter from Quarles's Mill, Grant told Meade to instruct "Warren and Wright to withdraw all their teams and artillery, not in position, to the north side of the river. . . . Send that belonging to General Wright's corps as far on the road to Hanover Town as it can go, without attracting attention to the fact." Sheridan, now back with Grant, placed his cavalry at vital surrounding crossings and bridges; he also carried the pontoons. Lee was not unaware of what was afoot, wiring Richmond, "The enemy retired to the north side of the North Anna last night." [2]

The route of the Army of the Potomac was not one that Grant liked:

The country we were now in was a difficult one to move troops over. The streams were numerous, deep and sluggish, sometimes spreading out into swamps grown up with impenetrable growths of trees and underbrush. The banks were generally low and marshy, making the streams difficult to approach except where there were roads and bridges.

Hanover Town is about twenty miles from Richmond. There are two roads leading there; the most direct and shortest one crossing the Chickahominy at Meadow Bridge, near the Virginia Central Railroad, the second going by New and Old Cold Harbor. A few miles out from Hanover Town there is a third road by way of Mechanicsville to Richmond. New Cold Harbor was important to us because while there we both covered the roads back to White House (where our supplies came from), and the roads southeast over which we would have to pass to get to the James River below the Richmond defences.[3]

Hanovertown was no garden spot on the map of Virginia. All that remained of the prosperous Page plantation once located here was an abandoned warehouse. But Grant had moved along the base of a triangle pointing toward Richmond with an efficiency that even the Confederates admired. The heavy foliage that disgruntled Grant left Lee with "only the vaguest information" concerning Federal movements.[4] Meanwhile Sheridan's horse soldiers reconnoitered toward Mechanicsville to ascertain Lee's position, and at Hawes's Shop, where the middle road branched off the direct road to Richmond, encountered Confederate cavalry "dismounted and partially intrenched." Not until Custer arrived with a brigade that evening (May 28) could the Rebels be budged. Grant wrote that "Our troops had to bury the dead, and found that more Confederate than Union soldiers had been killed." [5]

Next day the Federals still hunted for Lee's position. With only Burnside held in reserve, Grant sent Wright's corps to Hanover Court House, renowned as the birthplace of Patrick Henry. Hancock's corps moved toward Totopotomoy Creek, and Warren's corps remained on the Shady Grove Church Road. The Union forces advanced about three miles on the left, "with but little fighting," yet there was a definite "appearance of a movement past our left flank, and Sheridan was sent to meet it."

On May 30 Hancock found the enemy "strongly fortified" on the Totopotomoy.[6]

New Jersey's Robert McAllister, mounted on "one of the U. S. old plugs" now that Charley cavorted in whatever heaven exists for horses, was part of the force that kept Grant in contact with Butler's army on the James and the Union's new base of supplies at White House on the Pamunkey. Lee had learned from Northern newspapers dated as early as May 13 that an effort would be made to uncork Butler from his bottle, since Grant wanted his two corps. Butler's troops were being recalled, the dispatches reputedly said, because "they are not strong enough to take Richmond, and too strong to be idle." [7] But Baldy Smith, who looked and talked like a Prussian field marshal, had not reached White House when on May 29 General McAllister wrote his wife from "trenches across the Pamunkey River, 15 miles from Richmond."

Two days now had passed since McAllister had left the North Anna; and of the twenty-six days the Virginia campaign had occupied him, he had been under fire during at least twenty. Fortunately, the past forty-eight hours had been quiet, for the time had come when nineteen regiments would be mustered out of the Army of the Potomac since their terms of service had expired. More went home than re-enlisted. But recruits were arriving continually, so that McAllister would write Ellen, "We are getting a large army here." Of the quality of the 900 "heavies" from Washington—so called because they served the heavy artillery—McAllister was not so certain; "they looked well drilled . . . for poor fighting and campaigning."

The previous night the New Jerseymen had thrown up breastworks, expecting an attack by Lee, but none developed. Now the Unionists with McAllister watched Burnside's IX Corps passing toward the front. Nobody could guess what would be Grant's next move, except that the Federals "can't go far to the front until they encounter the enemy." [8]

What Grant was doing, now that his army had encountered Lee along the Totopotomoy, was asking Halleck to send all the pontoons in Washington to City Point. He ordered General William (Baldy) Smith, who had been with Butler on the James, to move his troops to White House and start up the south bank of the Pamunkey (if possible, as early as three o'clock on the morning of May 31).[9]

Perhaps it was the sight of the ladies waving their handkerchiefs as the Army of Northern Virginia marched from the North Anna that made Lee rise above his fatigue and illness. Even though he wrote his orders from a room in a hospital near Atlee's, Lee had used Totopotomoy Creek to demonstrate how superbly he could disperse troops to cover all approaches to Richmond if Grant crossed the Pamunkey River. Both sides claimed victory in the seven hours of fighting at Hawes's Shop, sometimes called the Battle of Enon Church. Lee realized his lines could be stretched so thin they could be easily penetrated if Beauregard tarried in reinforcing him. "The result of this delay," Lee wrote Davis on May 30, "will be disaster." [10]

That day the bluecoats and graycoats tangled. Wright was placed on the right and Burnside on the left of Hancock's corps while Warren moved up near Huntley (Hundley) Corner on the Shady Grove Church Road. Sporadic skirmishing at first made the affair seem insignificant until evening, when Early hurled an attack on Warren. At first shock Warren fell back and Grant feared that his left flank might be turned. Hancock was ordered to launch a frontal assault and "carried and held the rifle-pits," while "Warren got his men up, repulsed Early, and drove him more than a mile." The Confederates blamed Early's bloody failure on poor reconnaissance or coordination; in either event, it was a defeat that stung.[11]

Grant simplified the situation as it existed on the night of May 30. Lee "substantially" had spread his lines from Atlee's on the Virginia Central "south and east to the vicinity of Cold Harbor." Grant had countered by placing Warren's V Corps on the Shady Grove Church Road as far as the Mechanicsville Road and three miles or so south of the Totopotomoy. Burnside and then Hancock were next on Warren's right, followed by Wright on the extreme right to within about six miles southeast of Hanover Court House. Two of Sheridan's cavalry divisions watched the Federal left front toward Cold Harbor.[12]

There were veterans in both armies that remembered this country all too well, for they had fought near Cold Harbor (Gaines's Mill) when in 1862 General George B. McClellan marched up the peninsula from Yorktown to attack Richmond. Lee, then fighting his first Confederate battle, had seared memories on Yankee minds that they would never forget; he had flung his assault directly at the Union center. Lanky Sam Wilkeson of the *New York Tribune* had reported the Federal debacle. "A motley mob started pellmell for the bridges. . . . Scores of riderless, terrified horses [dashed] in every direction . . . [with] the sublime cannonading, the clouds of battlesmoke and the sun just disappearing, large and blood-red. . . ."[13] The South had found its finest general.

McClellan's weakness was that whereas he possessed a warrior's mind, he could not see one of his "boys" fall without feeling a stab in the heart; it was not a weakness that Grant shared. Now, on May 30, 1864, with 108,000 pawns against Lee's 59,000,

Grant was like a chess player who still missed the key move before crying "checkmate." He was offering Smith's corps as bait to draw Lee eastward, whereupon he intended to fall upon Lee's left and cut him off from Richmond. So sure was Grant that the Confederate movements on the left "indicated the possibility of a design" to separate Smith from the Army of the Potomac that he promised Smith, "They will be so closely watched that nothing could suit me better than such a move."

The flaw in Grant's reasoning was the fact that Lee did not know Smith was then disembarking his troops at White House. Lee made no movement to the east. His lines from Atlee's to beyond Old Cold Harbor stretched nine miles. On one side or the other he was looking for a weak spot where at long last he could push Grant back. British General J. F. C. Fuller, whose personal military experience began in the Boer War and who set out to prove Grant was a blunderer and ended believing him a genius, has interpreted the Confederate leader's thinking on May 30 perfectly:

"Lee's plan was to hold Grant's front with the corps of Hill and Breckinridge; attack his centre with Early's; and pivoting [Richard H.] Anderson's on Hoke and Fitzhugh Lee at Cold Harbor, to roll up Grant's left." [14]

Unless Lee could know the whereabouts and precise activities of Baldy Smith, the Confederate strategy was eminently intelligent.

Of course Lee later would be severely criticized for not having covered Cold Harbor and the James against Smith's advance, but among Lee's contemporaries, as among later armchair generals, there were many who were quicker with their mouths than their minds. Sheridan, nearing Cold Harbor on May 31, found the place occupied and entrenched by Confederate cavalry and infantry. Sheridan met General Alfred Torbert with the 1st Division of Cavalry at George Custer's headquarters "and found that the two had already been talking over a scheme to capture

Cold Harbor." Sheridan thought highly of the plan and ordered Pennsylvania's Colonel John Irvin Gregg's brigade forward to support Torbert.

With New York's Wesley Merritt's reserves and Custer's brigades, Torbert took the direct road to Cold Harbor. Tom Devin's brigade of Torbert's division was sent along a left-hand road that should bring him on the rear of the enemy's line. Devin did not quite reach his objective and needed help from part of Custer's brigade. From behind breastworks "hastily constructed out of logs, rails and earth," the Confederates raked the Union men with a fire so heavy "it seemed impossible to withstand." Gregg had not yet appeared, and Sheridan was on the verge of quitting when Merritt proceeded to turn the enemy's left. A frontal attack broke the Confederate defense and drove them to three-quarters of a mile beyond the village.

With a smugness the occasion scarcely warranted, Sheridan boasted, "Cold Harbor was now mine." But the truth soon emerged—he was scared and maybe scared stiff. His nearest infantry support was about nine miles away. "My isolated position," he admitted, "therefore made me a little uneasy." He expected a reinforced enemy to return at any moment. Sheridan informed Meade that the cavalry would withdraw that evening. Meade fired back an order instructing Sheridan "at every hazard" to stay where he was.[15]

Grant complimented Sheridan for speedily turning "the rebel works against them." What this statement meant, of course, was that Little Phil had his boys move the jumble of log-and-rail entrenchments so that they faced now toward the Confederates. Luckily no assault came that night. Grant by now had divined Lee's plan: to turn the Federal left flank and so separate Grant's army from its base and Smith's reinforcements. Wright's VI Corps was ordered to march that night to Sheridan's relief, but the darkness and distance prevented him from reaching Cold Harbor before nine o'clock on the morning of June 1.[16]

By then Sheridan had been twice assaulted. But his dismounted troops were not surprised, for during the night, as they distributed ammunition boxes and waited, they could hear their foe "giving commands and making preparations to attack."

At daylight, infantry under General Joseph B. Kershaw, who now led General Lafayette McLaws's division, advanced down the Bethesda Church road on Sheridan's right. Actually the attack was led by Colonel Lawrence M. Keitt, whose political and social eminence in South Carolina was not matched by his military knowledge. Sheridan could see Keitt riding recklessly forward on his horse and knew what to do: "he was permitted to come close up to our works, and when within short range such a fire was opened on him from our horse-artillery and [Spencer] repeating carbines that he recoiled in confusion. . . ."

Little Phil understated the situation. Keitt's regiment broke. In endeavoring to rally his men, the South Carolinian fell, mortally wounded. Thereafter, throughout the Confederate force, panic raced from unit to unit. Whether or not, as Freeman has suggested, at this moment Sheridan might have shattered the Confederate right wing if he had counterattacked vigorously is a conjecture no one can prove; but no one could dispute Freeman's conclusion: "After their repulse on the morning of June 1, the Confederates in their turn began to put between them and the enemy every tin cup of dirt that could be scraped from the loamy soil." [17]

The war clouds darkening over Cold Harbor found Richmond stoically politicking for whatever the future might bring. Rebel War Clerk Jones recorded on May 28 that the Secretary of the Treasury, Christopher G. Memminger, and "certain members of Congress have in readiness the means of sudden flight," and, later, that Congress "passed a bill increasing the compensation of themselves 100 per cent." [18]

Jones was almost overwhelmed by a train of cars, laden with provisions for the army, that remained on Broad Street and was "visited hourly by wagons from the army, now in the immediate vicinity." May ended in Richmond with a hot, clear day. For twenty hours soldiers under Beauregard marched down Main Street toward the road to Williamsburg. All local troops, including the young and aged, were alerted to stand ready to advance "at a moment's warning, this evening or night." No longer could anyone doubt that the "GREAT BATTLE" impended.[19]

Approaching the battles around Cold Harbor, a confident Grant felt thoroughly oriented to how the Army of the Potomac fought. He knew that at "every change of position or halt for the night," the troops would stack their arms and pile up a breastwork, behind which they would dig a ditch. The ditch served two functions: the dirt strengthened the breastwork and the depression increased the elevation in front of the soldiers and so improved their marksmanship. "It was wonderful how quickly they could in this way construct defences of considerable strength," Grant said.

But the general in chief found a greater marvel in the way the men of the telegraph and signal corps operated. Reels of wire weighing 200 pounds (insulated so that messages could be transmitted in a storm, on the ground, and underwater) were hoisted onto the backs of mules. Behind each pack team came wagons with light poles with iron-spiked ends that could be used for stringing the wire whenever a tree or fence post was not available. Each brigade was so equipped, and the key operators remained with the same headquarters unless specifically ordered elsewhere. "In a few minutes longer time than it took a mule to walk the length of its coil," Grant recalled, "telegraphic communication would be effected between all the headquarters of the army. No orders ever had to be given to establish the telegraph." [20]

At Cold Harbor the troopers in the Army of the Potomac would reveal still other characteristics. An astonished Horace Porter found the men in one regiment handy at needlework.

The soldiers not only were sewing up rents in their coats but also were pinning their names and addresses to the backs of these garments "so that their dead bodies might be recognized upon the field, and their fate made known to their families." [21] General Robert McAllister found men bathing in a millpond while whizzing shells passed overhead.[22] And Colonel Theodore Lyman of Meade's staff spoke with outright exasperation:

> To-day has been entirely quiet, our pickets deliberately exchanging papers, despite orders to the contrary. These men are incomprehensible —now standing from daylight to dark killing and wounding each other by thousands, and now making jokes and exchanging newspapers! You see them lying side by side in the hospitals, talking together in that serious prosaic way that characterizes Americans. The great staples of conversation are the size and quality of rations, the marches they have made, and the regiments they have fought against. All sense of personal spite is sunk in the immensity of the contest.[23]

On June 1—the day Sheridan's cavalrymen mortally wounded the reckless Keitt at Cold Harbor—War Clerk Jones awoke in Richmond at 7:30 A.M. to the clatter of cannon and musketry northeast of the city. Around noon this noise ceased "or else the hum of the city drowned the sounds of battle." [24]

Very likely the noises of the city disguised from Jones the rising crescendo of the afternoon's fighting. Sometime between three-thirty and four o'clock the Federals struck furiously in an effort to separate Anderson's right from Hoke's left. Horatio Wright's Federal VI Corps, moving in to take over Sheridan's trenches, came over the breastworks of logs, rails, and dirt with a bruising onslaught. There was no question but that the Confederate flank began to bulge. If Baldy Smith would arrive now with his XVII Corps of some 10,000 men, a breakthrough was within reach. Well might Wright ask, Where in God's name was the XVII Corps?

And well might Baldy have asked, Where was the XVII Corps supposed to be? Since landing his forces at White House, Baldy had been engaged in a game of military ring-around-a-rosy—the result of not one but *two* mistakes in orders from Grant's headquarters. Who was responsible for these blunders has never been definitely decided. The first of these orders, reaching Baldy on the afternoon of May 31, directed him to march to "New Castle" on the Pamunkey instead of Cold Harbor. Then the second erroneous dispatch, arriving on the morning of June 1, told Baldy to change his destination to New Castle Ferry. The men of the XVII Corps had cause to grumble if, as seems probable, they were foolishly marched off without their breakfasts.

Finally the correct order reached Baldy and led him to Cold Harbor. His troops were tired after tramping twenty-five miles. All through these hours, while Wright waited for Smith, the Confederates strengthened their defenses. Whereas the Federals now held the village of Old Cold Harbor, they could not turn or break the Confederate right, a result for which luck and not Lee's generalship deserved the credit.[25] McAllister's brief letter to his family reflected the over-all Federal bewilderment: "We have thrown up works, had constant fighting, and stormed and took the enemy's outer works yesterday [May 31] with our Division. This morning we have left them for some movements. I know not why. . . ."[26]

In Richmond, War Clerk Jones called the fighting on June 1 "heavy skirmishing" and not a general engagement. The 2nd passed quietly until five o'clock, when Jones added to his diary, "Heavy and quick cannonading heard some eight or ten miles east of the city. It continued until night, when it was raining and cold. . . ."[27] Had Smith arrived in sufficient time yesterday, Jones might not have spent the day in the capital.

"What are your views about tomorrow?" Meade asked Grant on the night of June 1. "I think the attack should be ordered as soon as Hancock is within supporting distance." Warren, Meade thought, should attack with Burnside standing ready if Warren required reinforcements.

Grant agreed.[28]

The action on June 2 centered around Cold Harbor. Again the spinning wheel of military fortune stopped on Lee's number, for at nightfall Cadmus Wilcox's division was within half a mile of the Chickahominy, an excellent position for defense because any frontal approach would be obstructed by thickets and marshes. What Lee intended, quite naturally, was to make his lines conform to Grant's. The Union general in chief planned an attack for the afternoon, then postponed it until morning. Meanwhile Federal cavalrymen amused themselves by tearing up rails of the Virginia Central. But the important factor was that Lee had been given an opportunity to strengthen Confederate defenses.[29]

X

Cold Harbor—
Grant Loses Patience

J. F. C. Fuller has sensed the pathos of the dilemma that confronted Grant on June 3. With the delegates already traveling to the National Union Convention, Grant's political judgment told him that Lincoln, like the mass of people in the North, wished a quick victory in Virginia. For thirty days, as Fuller has observed, Grant "had wrestled with the most noted general of the Confederacy," driving him from the Rapidan to the Chickahominy, in an area "as unsuited to offensive action as it was well suited to the defensive." Twice Grant had tried to turn Lee's flanks and failed. The Union's commander faced the hardest of all military realities—he had run out of space for maneuvering. If he withdrew from the field, could not that abandonment of his campaign be interpreted in the North as a dreadful disaster? The alternative—to assault Lee frontally—was fraught with terrible risks, but Grant decided to take it.[1]

After days of blistering heat, a cool and gentle rain was falling when at four o'clock War Clerk Jones awoke on the morning of June 3 to rattling windows and "an incessant roar of artillery." [2] Horace Porter, riding two miles from headquarters, branded as "gross slander" a reported weakness of morale among the Federals after so many days of fighting.[3]

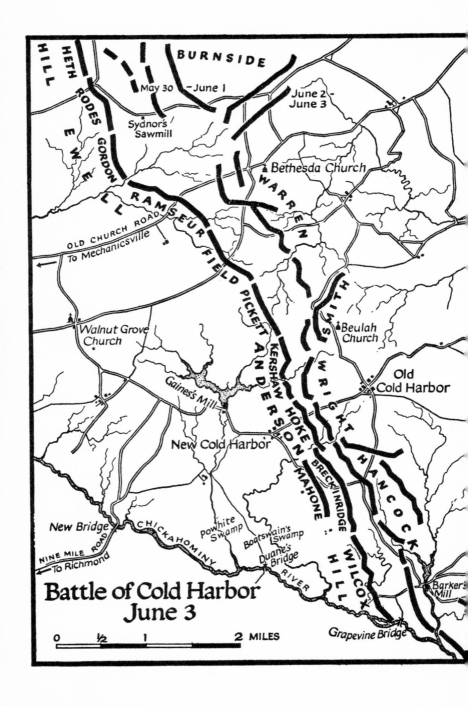

Battle of Cold Harbor
June 3

HETH
HILL

RODES

EWELL

GORDON

BURNSIDE

May 30 — June 1

Sydnor's
Sawmill

June 2 –
June 3

Bethesda Church

WARREN

RAMSEUR

OLD CHURCH ROAD
To Mechanicsville

FIELD

PICKETT

Walnut Grove
Church

Gaines's Mill

ANDERSON

KERSHAW

HOKE

SMITH

Beulah
Church

Old
Cold Harbor

WRIGHT

New Cold Harbor

BRECKINRIDGE

MAHONE

HANCOCK

New Bridge

NINE MILE ROAD
To Richmond

CHICKAHOMINY

Powhite
Swamp

Boatswain's
Swamp

Duane's
Bridge

RIVER

WILCOX
HILL

Barker's
Mill

Grapevine Bridge

0   ½   1   2 MILES

The Union attack, originally planned for four-thirty, was delayed perhaps as long as half an hour. Grant, who would belong to history if only for the mistakes he made this day, was misled by an assault by Jubal Early's corps on his right and concluded that Lee must be most vulnerable in his position around New Cold Harbor. Here he would resume his "hammering." The Confederates joked that the Yanks were like mosquitoes—where one was caught, two appeared [4]—but the Rebel banter vanished when the rumble of the Federal cannon spread from the heights of the Chickahominy far over to the Confederate left, a front of at least 4,000 feet. To Fuller, who believed that bullets and shells rather than masses of men won on a modern battlefield, Grant was doomed by too little firepower on so lengthy a front.[5]

William Swinton, historian of the Army of the Potomac, watched "the first gray light of dawn struggling through the clouds" as the men of the Federal II, VI, and XVIII Corps came forward through a murderous frontal and enfilade fire before being forced to take protection some thirty to fifty yards from the Confederate works. How long did the entire advance last? Eight minutes, ten?

In that little period [one eyewitness said], more men [7,000 Federals, 1,500 Confederates] fell bleeding ... than in any other like period of time throughout the war. A strange and terrible feature of this battle was that as the three gallant corps moved on, each was enfiladed while receiving the full force of the enemy's direct fire in front. . . . Each corps commander reported and complained to General Meade that the other commanders, right or left, as the case might be, failed to protect him from enfilading fire by silencing batteries in their respective fronts. . . . The three corps had moved upon diverging lines, each directly facing the enemy in its immediate front, and the farther each had advanced the more its flank had become exposed.[6]

Without comprehending this grand "overview," horrible though it was, the full collapse of the Federal generalship at New Cold Harbor cannot be appreciated. Little acts of valor fail otherwise to attain their full magnificence. In one action, brigades of the II Corps actually slugged their way to an advanced position but were overwhelmed before they could turn three heavy guns on the Confederates. The division of General John Gibbon tramped through a loosely defended area of swamp and planted the regimental colors of the 164th New York on the main Rebel works, but Gibbon's flanks were unprotected and the cost of his momentary glory was high—65 officers and 1,032 men killed and wounded.

Certainly Lee did not realize that he verged on victory in "his last great battle in the field" when at eight o'clock Confederate Postmaster General John H. Reagen and Judge James Lyons rode out to evaluate the true situation. They found Lee alone in his headquarters tent.

"General," Reagen asked, "if he breaks your line, what reserves have you?"

"Not a regiment," Lee replied, "and that has been my condition ever since the fighting commenced on the Rappahannock. If I shorten my lines to provide a reserve, he will turn me; if I weaken my lines to provide a reserve, he will break them." [7]

No official report can tell adequately the battle of Cold Harbor or estimate its consequences. The Confederates, many of whom had been subsisting on sassafras roots and wild grapes, fought splendidly. And so, too, did the troops in blue. Together their scarred memories held the full truth of Cold Harbor.

James N. Nichols, a captain in the 48th New York Volunteers, who called themselves Perry's Saints, remembered the excitement when the cry came, "Charge bayonets!" The 48th New York scampered across the field to the nearest enemy rifle pits, which were easily occupied. "It was a dreadful place to hold," Nichols wrote afterward. The Rebels opened with a deadly flanking fire. Repeated appeals to the 47th New York to come to the aid of Perry's Saints were ignored. So in the end, when the Confederates came with a rush, there was only one choice for Nichols and his 48th New York: "The enemy was fairly upon us and, before we could gather ourselves, someone without authority had called out to retreat. Back through the woods we went, broken and dispirited. . . ." [8]

That was one picture of Cold Harbor. General Robert McAllister drew a second: "Terable [sic] fighting, the likes of which was never known. The Jersey troops all fight well. The Rebel prisoners say that they are tired and hope it will be stoped [sic] soon. We took a large number of prisoners today. . . ." [9]

Colonel William Oates of the 15th Alabama Infantry, who had seen Union forces under Burnside slaughtered at Marye's Heights at Fredericksburg (December 13, 1862), still could not believe what his eyes beheld:

Just before I could see the sun, I heard a volley in the woods, saw the Major running up the ravine in the direction of Anderson's brigade, which lay to the right of Law's, and the skirmishers running in, pursued by a column of the enemy ten lines deep, with arms at a trail, and yelling "Huzzah! huzzah!" I ordered my men to take arms and fix bayonets. Just then I remembered that not a gun in the regiment was loaded. I ordered the men to load and the officers each to take an ax and stand to the works. I was apprehensive that the enemy would soon be on our works before the men could load.

As Capt. Noah B. Feagin and his skirmishers crawled over the works I thought of my piece of artillery. I called out: "Sergeant, give them double charges of canister; fire, men, fire!" The order was obeyed with alacrity. The enemy were within thirty steps. They halted and began to dodge, lie down, and recoil. The fire was terrific from my regiment, the Fourth Alabama on my immediate right, and the Thirteenth Mississippi on my left, while the piece of artillery was fired more rapidly and better handled than I ever saw one before or since. The blaze of fire from it at each shot went right into the ranks of our assailants and made frightful gaps through the dense mass of men. They endured it but for one or two minutes, when they retreated, leaving the ground covered with their dead and dying. There were 3 men in my regiment killed, 5 wounded. My piece of artillery kept up a lively fire on the enemy where they halted in the woods, with shrapnel shell.

After the lapse of about forty minutes another charge was made by the Twenty-third and Twenty-fifth Massachusetts regiments, in a column by divisions, thus presenting a front of two companies only. Bryan's Georgia brigade came up from the rear and lay down behind Law's. The charging column, which aimed to strike the Fourth Alabama, received the most destructive fire I ever saw. They were subjected to a front and flank fire from the infantry, at short range, while my piece of artillery poured double charges of canister into them. The Georgians loaded for the Alabamians to fire. I could see the dust fog out of a man's clothing in two or three places at once where as many balls would strike him at the same moment. In two minutes not a man of them was standing. All who were not shot down had lain down for protection. One little fellow raised his head to look, and I ordered him to come in. He came on a run, the Yankees over in the woods firing at him every step of the way, and as he climbed over our works one shot took effect in one of his legs. They evidently took him to be a deserter. I learned from him that there were many more out there who were not wounded. This I communicated to Colonel Perry, who was again in command, General Law having been wounded in the head during the first assault; and thereupon Perry sent a company down a ravine on our right to capture them; they soon brought the colonel who led the charge, and about one hundred other prisoners. The colonel was a brave man. He said he had been in many places, but that was the worst.[10]

Except for Francis Barlow, who fought under Hancock and who defied the crash of artillery and musketry to slug his way through thicket and swamps, where he seized three fieldpieces and turned them on the Confederates, the Federals had very little success and even Barlow was forced to withdraw for lack of support. Otherwise the seizure of outer rifle pits seemed the limit of the general Federal advance.

At seven o'clock that morning from "Near Cold Harbor" Grant had notified Meade, "The moment it becomes certain that an assault cannot succeed, suspend the offensive; but when one does succeed, push it vigorously and if necessary pile in troops at the successful point from wherever they can be taken. I shall go to where you are in the course of an hour."

Not more than thirty minutes later Grant sensed the substantial failure of his effort. He sought the judgments of his corps commanders on each of the fronts. Hancock saw the enemy as too strong; Wright believed he could gain the enemy's lines with the cooperation of Hancock and Smith; Baldy thought a lodgment was possible but he spoke with lukewarm enthusiasm; only Burnside expressed any great optimism, which Warren thoroughly squelched. Grant accepted the inevitable, yet he was in no mood to credit Lee with any measure of material victory. Lee, despite heavy Federal losses, "was not cheered by the occurrence sufficiently to induce him to take the offensive." [11]

Richmond's citizens reacted as wildly as the anti-Lincoln press did bitterly to Lee's stunning success. The number of Federal casualties was shamelessly exaggerated. Grant was accused of not burying his dead, which was untrue, since he requested a truce for this purpose on June 7. Rumors in Richmond that day described Grant as "quite drunk yesterday" and as saying that if he failed to win after another try at Lee "the Confederacy might go to hell." More charitable than most, War Clerk Jones commented, "It must have been some other general." [12]

Horace Porter heard Grant admit handsomely his failure at Cold Harbor: "I regret this assault more than any one I have ever ordered." No advantages were gained, he said, that could justify the losses suffered. He—and he alone—was responsible, after which confession, Porter remarked, "the matter was seldom referred to in conversation." [13] On June 8—the day the National Union Convention in Baltimore nominated its candidates—Lincoln spent the morning at the War Department in constant telegraphic communication with Grant. He dashed to the White House for a hurried lunch and returned to the War Department.[14] After a month of incessant campaigning, including the fighting at Cold Harbor, the North had lost 50,000 men and, as far as it was possible to obtain accurate figures, the South had lost 32,000. In round figures, Grant had lost 41 per cent of his original strength and Lee had lost 46 per cent. Whereas Grant could retrieve these losses within a few weeks and talk cheerily of Cold Harbor as "not a death-blow but a mistake to be repaired," [15] Lee had no hope that he ever could regain his balance even though Grant talked humanely of surrendering his "bust-'em-up" tactics.

The Northern people, grumbled the *Washington Chronicle*, possessed no greater vice than their almost instantaneous over-optimism. "We need," editorialized the *Chronicle*, "something more of the old Roman temper that grimly welcomed a triumph, and in the darkest hour never despaired of the Republic." The *Chronicle* belabored the influx of embalmers who opened their mortuaries beside private houses, restaurants, and markets. Washington "stank like a charnel house." Stormed the *Chronicle*, "It insults the meanest animals to have their dead and food in juxtaposition." [16]

Lincoln refused to be disheartened or critical. Such disadvantages as had accrued, he seemed to agree with Grant, were "of short duration." [17]

XI

★ ═══════════════════

Counterpunch

Grant never faltered simply because ideas were new. If massed action did not work against Lee, he would turn to surprise. If he could not attack Lee's army, he would go after his supplies. Sheridan was sent with two divisions to Charlottesville, and David Hunter, whose relief of Sigel was like changing a pot for a kettle, was ordered to strike the enemy's rear. If no more was accomplished than diverting Lee's attention, that fact was of the utmost importance at this time,[1] for Grant now intended, if necessary, to defy most of the bookish rules of war.

According to General Adam Badeau, Grant embarked on an operation which, in danger and difficulty, "transcended" any the general in chief ever had attempted. Grant proposed nothing less than withdrawing his army "within forty yards of the enemy's lines." Grant's objective was Petersburg, which meant crossing the swamps of the Chickahominy and then the wide, tidal James River. One hundred and fifty miles must be covered in transferring Grant's base of supplies from White House to City Point.

The whole plan of the national commanders at this juncture [Badeau wrote] assumed magnificent proportions. Sherman was advancing towards Atlanta and the sea, and [Edward R. S.] Canby had been ordered to begin the attack against Mobile to meet him, so that the rebel forces west of the mountains were all engaged; Hunter was moving up the Valley of Virginia; [General George] Crook [an old Indian fighter] and Averill [William S. Averell] were converging from the west and south-west, to cut off entirely the supplies reaching Richmond from these directions; Sheridan was advancing to complete the destruction and isolation on the north, while Grant himself moved with the bulk of his forces against Petersburg and the southern railroads. . . .[2]

Grant obviously resented Lee.

His praise, [Grant wrote] was sounded throughout the entire North after every action he was engaged in: the number of his forces was always lowered and that of the National forces exaggerated. He was a large, austere man, and I judge difficult of approach to his subordinates. To be extolled by the entire press of the South after every engagement, and by a portion of the press North with equal vehemence, was calculated to give him the entire confidence of his troops and to make him feared by his antagonists. It was not an uncommon thing for my staff-officers to hear from Eastern officers, "Well, Grant has never met Bobby Lee yet." There were good and true officers who believe now that the Army of Northern Virginia was superior to the Army of the Potomac. . . .[3]

At no time would Grant accept this proposition. Lee neither overawed nor frightened him. What, momentarily, Grant feared was the possibility that Lee, "with his shorter distance to travel and his bridges over the Chickahominy and the James," might fall on Butler and his troops before the Army of the Potomac could come to the rescue. Likewise, Lee might well release forces to beleaguer Hunter's approach to Lynchburg. Grant relied on "Lee's not seeing my danger as I saw it." [4]

Sheridan was sent to break up the Virginia Central Railroad and the James River Canal, routes of great importance in supplying the Army of Northern Virginia and the people of Richmond (after which Sheridan was expected to rescue the hapless Hunter). Orders were issued to take up the iron from the

York River Railroad and place it on boats for ultimate shipment to Grant's new headquarters at City Point. Hunter reported a successful engagement near Staunton. Lee, seeing in Sheridan's cavalry activities a threat to Confederate communications and supplies, sent most of his cavalry after Little Phil, while Early, with Ewell's entire corps, was dispatched to deal with Hunter.

Wading through swamp, water, and mud, Federal cavalrymen stretched pontoon bridges across the Chickahominy. Warren's corps was first to cross and with cavalry help was expected to hold the roads from Richmond. To Grant's delight, "No attempt was made by the enemy to impede our march." Hancock neared the James River at Charles City Court House on June 13. Wright's and Burnside's corps crossed the Chickahominy that same evening and next night, by boat and bridge, also put the James behind them. The wagon trains moved farther east by Windsor Shades Landing and Cole's Ferry.

On the night of June 14 Grant steamed to Bermuda Hundred to discuss personally with Butler the purpose of his movement to seize and hold Petersburg, which he considered far more important than Richmond, since at Petersburg the Union could clutch "the arteries of the Confederacy at the throat." Grant acted in exuberant spirits. Reinforcements had swelled the Army of the Potomac to 115,000, or a thousand less than its number when the Virginia campaign had started in the Wilderness. He was at that very moment outwitting Lee, and doing so under the noses of the Confederate spies who riddled the countryside.[5]

Lee's failure during this Federal movement across the James was not the fault of the smallness of his army, now about 64,000 including the 14,000 replacements he had received during the campaign. Lee's weakness was in judging Grant, in a military sense, as a sort of lumbering, unimaginative ox. On June 15, 16, and 17, Lee did nothing while Grant led his army into a new position with skilled flanking movements. With

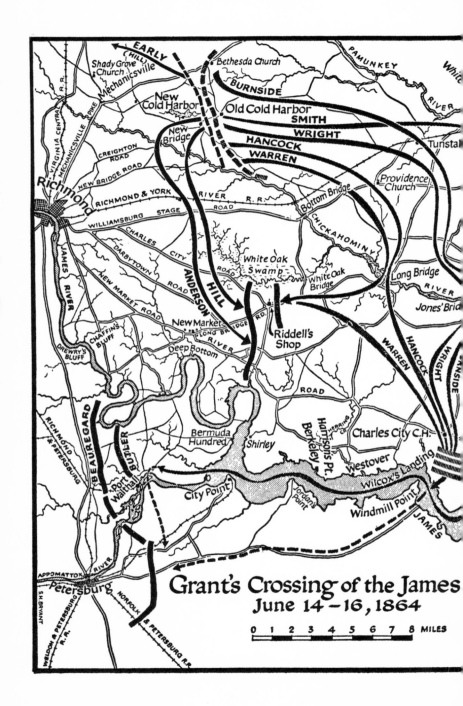

Grant's Crossing of the James
June 14–16, 1864

0 1 2 3 4 5 6 7 8 MILES

abundant opportunities to strike Grant in detail and in flank, Lee simply remained militarily comatose, expecting a vicious attack where he then stood. Growled the Rebel General Edward P. Alexander, "Thus the last, and perhaps the best, chances of Confederate success, were not lost in the repulse of Gettysburg, nor in any combat of arms. They were lost during three days of lying in camp, believing that Grant was hemmed in by the broad part of the James below City Point, and had nowhere to go but to come and attack us. The entire credit for the strategy belongs, I believe, to Grant." [6]

Butler agreed with Grant that the attack on Petersburg should be led by Baldy Smith. How many books on the art of war had been crammed into Baldy's head no one could count, but out of this welter of technical knowledge came Baldy's belief that as a general Butler was a political joke and that Grant had not known how to fight at Cold Harbor. Even so, Smith was adequately strengthened for the task assigned him. Six thousand troops were added to Baldy's command—about 2,500 troops under General August V. Kautz and some 3,500 colored troops under Edward W. Hinks—so that, in round figures, Smith's attacking force was between 16,000 and 18,000. With no more than six miles to advance, Baldy was expected to move up on the night of June 14 and be prepared to assault the thinly held Confederate lines at Petersburg at daybreak. If Smith had obeyed verbal orders, Grant contended then and still believed when he raced death to finish his *Memoirs*, Petersburg "could have been easily captured." There were fewer than 2,500 trained defenders and some slipshod irregulars to contest a Federal assault. A series of strong redans, connected by rifle pits, if properly manned, Grant said, "could have held out against any force that could have attacked them, at least until reinforcements could have got up from the north of Richmond." [7]

But Baldy Smith approached Petersburg in a sulky mood, setting great store on the fact that Butler had not supplied him with a written plan of action. Hancock was ordered to support Smith but dallied, awaiting rations that Meade promised but never sent, yet at least if Hancock was somewhat fuzzy-headed he had the excuse of being confined to an ambulance because "of the breaking out afresh of the wound he had received at Gettysburg."

Baldy reached Petersburg about 10 o'clock on the morning of June 15 and, determined to be correct in every step, wandered around judging the strength of the city's defenses. Finally, about 7:00 P.M., Smith assaulted "with the colored troops" and after two hours held five redans with their artillery and connecting rifle pits. Hancock joined him and was asked to relieve the men in the trenches. Otherwise, in Baldy's judgment, "it was wiser to hold what we had than . . . to lose what we had." Bright moonlight illuminated the field of battle. Baldy had no excuse for not taking the city that night, even without Hancock, and his failure to do so, as Fuller saw the situation, probably prolonged the war six months and added another 100,000 names to the casualty lists.

The dapper Creole, P. G. T. Beauregard, turned Petersburg from a crushing defeat into a siege that allowed the Confederacy to buy time for recollecting its wits, and he did so virtually singlehandedly, for as late as June 17 Lee insisted that he still had "no information" to substantiate the claim of Grant having crossed the James. Fuller spoke extravagantly of Beauregard's "consummate skill" under the circumstances:

He was a man of enterprise and daring, highly imaginative, for he could often foresee the movements and actions of his enemy. In his present situation, he measured up Smith with extreme accuracy; he bluffed him into believing that Petersburg was strongly held, by making a great noise with his artillery, and by boldly throwing forward his skirmishers as if they were supported by strong columns in rear.[8]

On June 18 a telegram from Beauregard told Lee that he was confronted "by the whole of Grant's army." Lee still doubted Beauregard, replying that it was "only upon your representations" that he would move to Petersburg. Investing this city was hardly what Grant had wished; but, with a bulldog grip, he was going to hold fast to Lee.

The moaning, lovelorn Wash Roebling found this unexpected turn of events heavy to bear; and in crisp sentences his letters to Emily Warren revealed his dislike for this kind of war. Thus: "It is the same old story every day: kill, kill, kill." And again: "I am all dirty, ragged and I might say lousy. There isn't a brass button on my coat, I haven't had a shirt collar on since we left Culpeper and when my only shirt is washed I lie abed." And later: "People talk about getting used to fighting and to battles, but I don't see it in that light." Later yet: "Your brother G. K. [Warren] now spends half his waking hours in cursing the damned fate that keeps him away from his wife." And finally: "Nothing but hot sandy fields surround us, and the woods are even worse as there isn't a breath of air stirring there. Luckily for us the same sun shines on the rebs and I don't think they can stand it any better even if they do come from the South." [9]

No one supported Grant more loyally than Edward McMasters Stanton, and a letter from Sherman, who was stoically pounding his way toward the conquest of Atlanta, pleased the Secretary of War.

"If General Grant can sustain the confidence, the esprit, the pluck of his army, and impress the Virginians with the knowledge that the Yankees can and will fight them fair and square, he will do more good than the capture of Richmond or any strategic movements, and this is what Grant is doing." [10]

Stanton sent his assistant, Charles A. Dana, to see Grant at City Point. Dana reported that Grant held no political ambitions, an important point to Stanton. Moreover, Dana told Stanton, except for "nuisance raids," Lee could no longer be considered a threat to the North.

"All of his [Lee's] railroads have been broken up, all of north-west Virginia is destitute, deprived not only of supplies, but of laborers, so that the harvests which have been put into the ground . . . cannot be harvested." The situation in Virginia, Dana said, "is becoming more gloomy from day to day." [11]

There was no report that Stanton would be happier to receive.

Jefferson Davis excelled in nurturing a grudge. The bad feeling between the President and General Joseph E. Johnston had now reached a point where Lydia Johnston no longer spoke to Varina Davis. It was no secret the President believed that Johnston's lack of aggressiveness against Grant had cost the Confederacy the city of Vicksburg, and it was equally plain that Davis would have preferred giving the leadership of the Army of Tennessee to William J. Hardee, who then commanded the Department of South Carolina, Georgia, and Florida.

But Johnston claimed friends, both in and out of Richmond, who had no intention of seeing him shunted aside. Outstanding in this group was Congressman Henry S. Foote, a former governor of Mississippi unafraid of exchanging acid remarks with Davis or his principal supporter, Congressman William G. Swann of Tennessee. A tense Cabinet meeting reflected this conflict. Secretary of War James A. Seddon, confessing disappointment in Johnston's "absence of enterprise," still felt that "Joe" should be given another chance. A glowering pinched look of disgust on the face of Judah P. Benjamin revealed the Secretary of State's distrust of Johnston's "tendencies to defensive strategy and a lack of knowledge of the environment." The general belief, though never proved, had Lee making the ultimate selection. Naturally, one by one, these criticisms reached Johnston, who could not "perceive that our cause will be benefitted by my being thought worse than I am." [12]

Johnston tried to reach a cordial accommodation with Davis based upon "an aggressive movement." The General believed that the Federal forces in Tennessee at Missionary Ridge were stronger than the War Department imagined. Quite frankly Johnston declared that defeat beyond the Tennessee would probably prove ruinous. It would result in the loss of his army, the occupation of Georgia by the enemy, the "piercing of the Confederacy in its vitals," and the surrender of all southwestern territory. The prospect chilled Davis, who was willing to approve of any plan that would force the Federals to evacuate the Tennessee Valley.[13]

Redheaded Sherman was the unpredictable link in everybody's strategy, probably including his own. A West Point education had been wasted on him, except for the slight chance it gave him to chase Seminoles in Florida. He feared the responsibility of an independent command and begged Lincoln not to give him one; placed on his own in Kentucky, his hallucinations of overwhelming enemy forces produced an extravagant request for extraordinary reinforcements and led his son to race home with a newspaper, the *Cincinnati Gazette,* that declared "Papa is Crazy." At this point Sherman could have been washed out of the army, but numerous friends, none more so than Grant, nursed him back to military health as a bold, aggressive, imaginative commander.

In a country of long mountain ranges, cut by few roads and paths, Johnston could not have asked for a worse opponent. Sherman was like a professional football quarterback who employed screen plays and short end runs in an irresistible advance toward his goal. Davis could not understand the strategy but still shivered at the consequences:

> Thus, from Dalton [Georgia] to Resaca, from Resaca to Adairsville, from Adairsville to Alatoona (involving by the evacuation of Kingston the loss of Rome with its valuable mills, foundries, and large quantities of military stores), from Alatoona to Kenesaw, from Kenesaw to the Chattahoochie, and then to Atlanta; retreat followed retreat, during seventy-four days of anxious hope and bitter disappointment . . . at last the Army of Tennessee fell back within the fortifications of Atlanta . . .[14]

Davis failed to credit how under harrowing conditions Johnston had kept his army intact and in good spirits and, if necessary, might force Sherman to follow him to the shores of the Gulf of Mexico. Convinced of his sagacity in his doubts about Johnston, Davis battered him with telegrams asking when he intended to fight. Finally on July 18 he replaced Johnston with General John B. Hood. With his sad eyes of a bloodhound, Hood had fought in several major engagements and carried a crippled left arm as a souvenir of Gettysburg and the stump of a right leg as a souvenir of Chickamauga.

Hood was a good administrator whose defenses were masterful, but on offense he was a shameful bumbler. He fought Sherman from July 22 to August 26 before realizing that the wily Federal redhead had virtually surrounded him and the immediate evacuation of Atlanta had become inevitable.

XII

Wigwam by a Lake

As August neared an end it was clear that Sherman would win Atlanta. Morever, with the fall of Fort Gaines and Fort Morgan (August 7 and 23), the North won the Battle of Mobile Bay. One hundred and four guns and 1,500 prisoners were captured when this last remaining major Southern port fell. The Union found another hero in tough old Admiral David G. Farragut, who had damned the torpedoes and steamed into the Bay as "the gray glimmer of dawn was just beginning to struggle through a dense fog" on August 12.[1]

Far from being cheered, professional Republicans were gloomier than they ever had been. Thurlow Weed, the party's shrewdest wheeler-dealer, wrote a tough letter to Secretary of State Seward on August 22. Mr. Lincoln's re-election was "an impossibility." Henry J. Raymond, the editor of the New York Times, agreed with Weed that "unless some prompt step" now be taken, "all is lost." The people were "wild" for peace but were told that the President "will only listen to terms of Peace on condition Slavery be 'abandoned.'" Something must be done, Weed urged, "to give the Administration a chance for its life."[2]

Raymond went straight to the source of the trouble. "The tide is setting strongly against us," he warned Lincoln. Why not compromise Jefferson Davis by proposing a peace conference? Raymond suggested. Davis would repel the offer and thus prove to the North that peace only could be obtained through another military victory. Lincoln must face the facts. Washburne wrote Raymond that "were an election to be held now in Illinois we should be beaten." Former Secretary of War Simon Cameron saw Pennsylvania "against us." Governor Oliver P. Morton believed that "nothing but the most strenuous efforts can carry Indiana." Raymond predicted that New York would be lost by 50,000 votes.[3]

On August 23 Lincoln had each member of his Cabinet sign a folded sheet of paper which, unread, the President placed in his desk drawer. He had written:

"This morning, as for some days past, it seems exceedingly probable that this administration will not be re-elected. Then it will be my duty to so co-operate with the President-elect, as to save the Union between the election and the inauguration; as he will have secured his election on such grounds that he cannot possibly save it afterwards." [4]

With the Democrats soon to meet for their nominating convention in Chicago, with their orators exhorting the North that peace could never be gained by the Republicans, and with presidential secretary John Nicolay predicting that "Hell is to pay," the moment was at least delicate for the erratic and strong-willed editor and publisher of the *New York Herald*, Horace Greeley, to impose his influence on the White House. On the authority of Confederate agents—dubious at best—the owlish Greeley had learned that Jefferson Davis had sent to the Canadian side of Niagara Falls, with credentials to arrange for a cessation of hostilities, the Honorable Clement C. Clay of Alabama and Jacob Thompson, who had been Attorney General in Buchanan's Cabinet. Greeley was obstinate in the belief that he could arrange terms of a peace.

Lincoln, far shrewder than the editor-publisher in reading the minds of Confederates, guessed quite accurately that Clay and Thompson had gone North to raise all the mischief they could. Clay had prepared the platform for the coming Chicago Convention, Lincoln reminded Greeley. They were not empowered to negotiate a peace. Lincoln quoted Clay: "The stupid tyrant who now disgraces the chair of Washington and Jackson could, any day, have peace and restoration of the Union; and would have them, only that he persists in the war merely to free the slaves." [5]

Greeley insisted and Lincoln reluctantly agreed to let him go. Jeremiah S. Black, Secretary of the Interior under Buchanan, accompanied Greeley—why, it is difficult to say, for in the present school of politics he was as much a babe in arms as anyone. Black was so pleased with what Greeley and he had accomplished that he not only wrote Stanton from Toledo, where he had contacted Thompson, but also paid a morning visit to the Secretary of War's home.

Black stated that no one could doubt that the people of the South wanted an armistice and peace. Naturally concessions must be made: Southern domestic affairs must be left undisturbed, their state debts honored, their soldiers rewarded. Slavery in the territories posed no quarrel. Doubtless they could do without a fugitive slave law. Stanton exploded. Who the hell was Black to pose as representing the government?

"The upshot of it all is," Stanton declared, "that you go for an armistice, which is nothing more and nothing else than South Carolina wanted when the rebellion began; you and I then opposed it as fatal to the government and our national existence. I still oppose it on the same ground." [6]

In the final analysis all the Niagara Falls affair achieved was breaking up a warm friendship between Stanton and Black.

In high spirits reporter Noah Brooks arrived on August 28 in the city on the shores of Lake Michigan. That monstrous Chicago structure, the Wigwam, where four years ago the

Republicans had started Lincoln down the path to national fame, now buzzed with excited Democrats. Trains on the Lake Shore tracks clanked by, filling the building with smoke and cinders. Thousands of spectators jammed the pit and derisively hooted "War Democrat!" at delegates like "Sunset" Cox of Ohio.

Although the imposing Horatio Seymour, the governor of New York who bobbed a dark-reddish, balding head when he spoke, was president of the convention, its hero was another Ohioan, Clement L. Vallandigham, a state legislator, a fanatical opponent of Lincoln, and a leading Copperhead organizer of the Knights of the Golden Circle. Lincoln had ordered Vallandigham banished to the Confederacy, where Jefferson Davis had no notion of how to use him; but the famous Copperhead had eased that problem by escaping via Nassau and Canada in order to attend the Chicago convention.

Modestly Vallandigham waited in the background while Seymour finished his opening address. Then, representing Ohio on the platform committee, he stepped forward amid admiring huzzahs. His was the key plank, that

after four years of failure to restore the Union by the experiment of war, during which, under the pretense of a military necessity or war power higher than the Constitution, the Constitution itself has been disregarded in every part ... the public welfare demands that immediate efforts be made for a cessation of hostilities with a view to an ultimate convention of the States, or other peaceable means to the end that at the earliest practicable moment peace may be restored on the basis of the Federal union of the States.[7]

Not altogether to the pleasure of Peace Democrats like Vallandigham, the presidential nomination went in a landslide to General George B. McClellan, and, Brooks reported, "men threw up their hats, and behaved as much like bedlamites as men usually do under such circumstances." A volley of cannon rocked the Wigwam. Vallandigham was again honored with "a terrific outburst," which he received "bland, smiling, and rosy," Senator

George H. Pendleton of Ohio was selected for vice-president, and the citizens of Chicago slept fretfully that night as the delegates made the rounds of the drinking establishments.

Once Lincoln believed in a man, no matter what the political consequences might be, he lived with his conviction. Thus on June 15 he wired Grant, "Have just read your despatch of 1 P.M. yesterday. I begin to see it. You will succeed. God bless you all." [8]

Lincoln exulted in the surrender of Atlanta—a victory which, politically, the President so desperately required. On September 3 he wrote Sherman, "The marches, battles, sieges, and other military operations that have signalized this campaign must render it famous in the annals of war, and have entitled those who have participated therein to the applause and thanks of the nation." [9]

A victorious Sherman heard again from Lincoln on September 19:

The state election of Indiana occurs on the 11th. of October, and the loss of it to the friends of the Government would go far towards losing the whole Union cause. The bad effect upon the November election, and especially the giving the State Government to those who will oppose the war in every possible way, are too much to risk, if it can possibly be avoided. . . . Indiana is the only important State, voting in October, whose soldiers cannot vote in the field. Any thing you can safely do to let her soldiers, or any part of them, go home and vote at the State election, will be greatly in point. They need not remain for the Presidential election, but may return to you at once. This is, in no sense, an order, but is merely intended to impress you with the importance, to the army itself, of your doing all you safely can, yourself being the judge of what you can safely do.[10]

August had been a steam box in Washington. Among the nerves most frayed were those belonging to Salmon P. Chase, who found himself replaced as Secretary of the Treasury by William Pitt Fessenden, chairman of the Senate Finance Committee.

The job would kill him, Fessenden asserted.

"Very well," Stanton replied. "You cannot die better than in trying to save your country."

Time. That was all the Democratic party needed, in Dana's judgment, to become hopelessly divided. Lincoln's triumph was certain, Dana seemed to think, with Sherman in the center of Georgia, destroying Jefferson Davis's "last major rail links between the southeast and the Mississippi Valley," and Grant with a secure base on the James "with short lines of communication." [11]

When next Lincoln wired a general it would be to say "God bless you" to Little Phil Sheridan.

XIII

In the Valley

One of the "nuisance raids" Dana had prophesied came sooner than either he or Stanton had expected. Jubal Early, bald and stooped, began romping across Virginia the first week of July. From the Valley, where General David Hunter had withdrawn his cavalry so far into West Virginia that he was of doubtful usefulness to anyone, Early's raiders turned back and crossed the Potomac.

Lieutenant Colonel George Hitchcock feared for the safety of Washington. Halleck, who could share anyone's apprehensions, including Hitchcock's, explained that he had reported the situation to Grant, who had not recommended taking any action. Therefore, Halleck contended, his hands were tied. A still fretful Hitchcock hastened to the White House, where he found a depressed President looking "quite paralyzed and wilted down." Lincoln had suffered his last criticism for meddling in tactical movements, Hitchcock heard.

Somehow an army had to be thrown together to stand against Early's hard-riding graycoats. Stanton's solution was to call for 100,000 militiamen from New York and Pennsylvania to serve for a hundred days. New York's Governor Horatio Seymour responded graciously; but, as the Secretary of War might have anticipated,

Pennsylvania's Governor Andrew Curtin was in one of his uppish moods. Curtin thought it was fine for the Federal government to pay and provision his militiamen, but otherwise Curtin intended to retain control over the men from Pennsylvania. Somehow Stanton's fist-pounding changed Curtin's mind. The troops from New York and Pennsylvania were placed under General Lew Wallace, a veteran of many campaigns who would owe his greatest claim to prominence as the author of *Ben Hur.*

Early, riding eastward toward Washington, easily overran western Maryland. Too late in recognizing the threat to Washington, Grant relieved James B. Ricketts's division of the VI Corps to support Wallace.[1]

Dug in on the banks of the Monocacy River, in Maryland, Wallace never had a chance—because Hunter's cavalry did not return from the west to support Wallace's rear and because Grant was too late in wiring Halleck to send the rest of the VI Corps and part of the XIX Corps to reinforce the defense of Washington and western Maryland. On July 9, Early's gray raiders, shouting and confident, reached the Monocacy River, just southwest of Frederick, Maryland.

Early found Wallace, with an infantry and cavalry brigade, reinforced by James B. Ricketts's division, entrenched and waiting. Early's plan was not completely formed when at noon he attacked. General John McCausland's Confederate cavalry brigade hit first. James B. Gordon's division followed. It was a battle uphill and over fences and past piled grain stacks—a regular fox hunt—before Gordon drove the Federals from their front two lines. Gordon, maneuvering to assault the third line, saw his men rush forward without receiving orders. The Federals were routed due to vicious attacks by Steve Ramseur's division and Robert Rodes's division across the Baltimore pike. Early, who had no wish to be overburdened by prisoners, did not press the charge too vigorously. Among the 6,050 Federal troops engaged, he had inflicted 1,880 casualties (including 1,188 missing). His own losses were not more than 700 among 14,000 engaged.

Early now was at the high point in his career. Never before had "Old Jube" done so well as, pressing his luck, he cut the telegraph wires connecting Washington to the north. Grimly, Stanton's clerks in the War Department sat with loaded muskets beside their desks.[2]

Secretary of the Navy Gideon Welles was shocked at what had happened. On July 9 he confided to his diary, "I learn nothing from the War Office, and am persuaded there is both neglect and ignorance there." On July 10, a Sunday, Welles added, "There has been no information to warn us of this near approach of the enemy, but my informant was so positive—and soon confirmed by another—that I sent to the War Department to ascertain the facts." And next day, like a drowning man going under for the third time, Welles bemoaned, "The Rebels are upon us. . . ."[3]

Actually Jubal Early, turning from Rockville to the Seventh Street pike that ran from Silver Spring into Washington, could not be sure of triumph. There had been no rain for several weeks; and this day (July 11) was "an exceedingly hot one, and no air stirring." Exhausted men fell by the wayside. As a result, Early was delayed much longer than he wished. Arriving in sight of Fort Stevens, he discovered that the defenses around Washington were not what he had been led to believe:

[Robert] Rodes' skirmishers were thrown to the front, driving those of the enemy to the cover of the works, and we proceeded to examine the fortifications in order to ascertain if it was practicable to carry them by assault. They were found to be exceedingly strong, and consisted of what appeared to be enclosed forts of heavy artillery, with a tier of lower works in front of each pierced for an immense number of guns, the whole being connected by curtains with ditches in front, and strengthened by palisades and abattis. The timber had been felled within cannon range all around and left on the ground, making a formidable obstacle, and every possible approach was raked by artillery. On the right was Rock Creek, running through a deep ravine which had been rendered impassable by the felling of the timber on each side, and beyond were the works on the Georgetown pike which had been reported to be the strongest of all. On the left, as far as the eye could reach, the works appeared to be of the same impregnable character. The position was naturally strong for defence, and the examination showed, what might have been expected, that every appliance of science and unlimited means had been used to render the fortifications around Washington as strong as possible. This reconnaissance consumed the balance of the day.[4]

Reputedly it was at Fort Stevens during this time that Oliver Wendell Holmes, then a captain on Wright's staff, did not recognize the distinguished visitor when he shouted at Lincoln, "Get down, you damn fool, before you get shot!" But Jubal Early was equally red-faced when he recognized how "broken down" many of his barefooted men were. One result which his raids in the Valley and Maryland had produced was to reduce his infantry "to about 8,000 muskets." Now, after two days of weary marching, men were dropping by the roadside with sunstroke. If he attacked the forts like the one Lincoln had inspected, Early could count on "not more than one-third of my force" plus about forty pieces of field artillery (the largest were 12-pounder Napoleons), besides what small amount of artillery the cavalry carried.

General McCausland, who had chased Hunter's Unionists from the Shenandoah, reported Georgetown too heavily guarded to be assaulted. Early worried over the signal station atop the Soldiers' Home that could detect every movement the Confederates made, right or left. Any attack on Washington's fortifications must be made "blindly," which Early believed "would have been worse than folly." Bitterly the General added, "If we had any friends in Washington, none of them came out to give us information, and this satisfied me that the place was not undefended." [5]

Welles was quite out of patience with what had occurred. He sneered at Halleck and Stanton as "the most alarmed men in Washington," and added:

I am sorry to see so little reliable intelligence. It strikes me that the whole demonstration is weak in numbers but strong in conception. . . . I am satisfied no attack is now to be apprehended on the city; the Rebels have lost a remarkable opportunity. But on our part there is neglect, ignorance, folly, imbecility, in the last degree. The Rebels are making a show of fight while they are stealing horses, cattle, etc., through Maryland. They might easily have captured Washington. Stanton, Halleck, and Grant are asleep or dumb.[6]

The rumor that Grant had sent two corps to Washington convinced Early that the Union's "whole army was probably in motion." Consequently the Confederate "reluctantly" surrendered any hope of capturing the national capital although he added, somewhat boyishly, that he "had arrived in sight of the Capitol, and given the Federal authorities a terrible fright." [7] Lee's chief criticism, which he voiced only to Early, was that he had "operated more with divisions than with your concentrated strength." But Early, often harsh and sarcastic in speech, had left a rather large body of detractors in Virginia. One was Governor William Smith, who frankly admitted to "some little unfriendliness in my relations with General Early." Smith accused Early of a succession of shortcomings: that he had been surprised, that his tactics were poor, that he had lost guns, that the soldiers no longer considered him "a safe commander." Lee vigorously defended Early against his critics; Early was the first of Lee's senior officers who had put his commanding general to this test; [8] but since Fort Stevens outside Washington had been strongly reinforced during the night, Early had acted discreetly in his withdrawal.

The first of the world's great modern wars that had begun in a wave of legally disputable emotionalism and would soon end in undernourished exhaustion now evolved into a new conflict over railroad logistics. Grant saw no advantage in attempting to storm Petersburg when by a siege he would have more men available to strike the Confederacy in a spot where it was most highly vulnerable. In this "war on the railways" Grant divided his attack against the two systems of carriers running out of Richmond and Petersburg.[9]

Of the lines leading from Richmond, both the Fredericksburg and the Richmond & York River railroads could be dismissed as already of virtual uselessness. Two other lines—the Virginia Central and the Richmond & Petersburg—could not be so easily brushed aside if Lee and the Confederacy were to survive. The Virginia Central, connecting Richmond with the produce of the Shenandoah Valley, was of vital importance unless Virginia wished to face a winter of agonizing starvation. Federal cavalry raids in June had torn up twenty-one miles of the Virginia Central; and the main line of the Richmond & Petersburg, needed for the rapid transferral of Confederate troops between these two cities, had been destroyed near Port Wathall Junction.

Lee at once realized that the Petersburg railroad could not be held and was willing to accept it as expendable. Its rolling stock and materials, he thought, might far better be sent to other roads. He had in mind three strategic routes: the Richmond & Danville, which had recently been connected with the Piedmont and thus had access to North Carolina; the Piedmont itself; and the Southside Railroad, which ran west from Petersburg to a junction with the Richmond & Danville at Burkeville, thus opening its route to Lynchburg where connection could be made with the Virginia & Tennessee and the Orange & Alexandria.

Confederate Secretary of War Seddon hated to yield the Petersburg, which at Weldon connected with the seaboard railroads of North Carolina. At least, Seddon thought, Lee might try to hold onto the Petersburg for the next three weeks until the wheat crop then being threshed could be delivered. The general demurred.

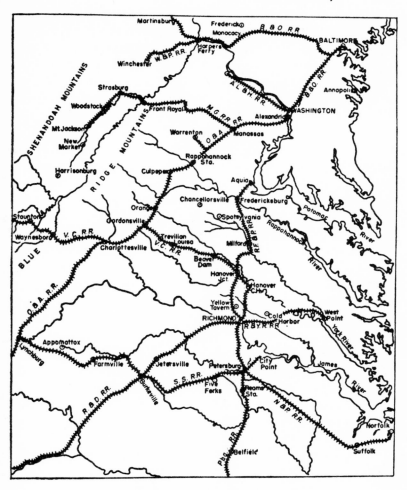

Railroads in Virginia, 1864–65

"If the Danville railroad cannot be made to supply our wants we shall inevitably suffer. . . . I see no way of averting the terrible disaster that will ensue." [10]

The Federals swept down on the railroads wherever they could. Some 7,500 cavalrymen under Generals James H. Wilson and

August V. Kautz struck the Petersburg at Reams's Station, burned the depot and thirteen cars, and tore up another stretch of track. Here Wilson and Kautz separated. At Ford's Station, on the Southside Railroad fourteen miles west of Petersburg, Wilson destroyed two trains of cars carrying cotton and furniture. Wilson turned back to Burkeville and wrecked about thirty miles of track. Meanwhile Kautz had left the crossing tracks on the Southside and Richmond & Danville in a shambles. Rejoining, Wilson and Kautz vented Federal wrath on the stations, tracks, turntables, and trestles of the Richmond & Danville. It was really no great trick destroying the thin rails by firing the ties on which they were mounted.

Lee could not permit this mischief to continue much longer. Wilson and Kautz returned to Reams's Station, expecting to find their own troops there. Instead they encountered Rebel infantry under General William Mahone, formerly a president of the Norfolk & Petersburg, who bore a special grudge against railroad wreckers. Fresh cavalry under Wade Hampton and Rooney Lee (Lee's second son) supported Mahone. They hit the surprised Federals with cyclonic velocity. Kautz was lucky to break through with a few regiments. Wilson lost his wagons and twelve cannon before he retreated down the railroad's west side at Jarratt's Station. In addition to his heavy casualties Wilson left behind about 1,000 prisoners and hundreds of Negroes who had joined the Federal caravan.[11]

Yet Wilson and Grant were undismayed. Almost exuberantly, the cavalry leader reported to his general that "every depot, turn-table, water-tank, and trestle-work between the Sixteen-Mile Turnout on the South Side Railroad to the Roanoke bridge on the Danville road was destroyed." [12] Grant believed that several weeks must pass before Lee could use any of his railroads.

Rations for the Army of Northern Virginia were cut in half. Inside Richmond, where War Clerk Jones found potatoes selling at $5 a quart and $160 a bushel, undeniable proof of inflation was provided as Congress debated a measure raising President Davis's wages since "he cannot subsist on his previous salary." The story was told that even if Richmond had to do without newspapers, typesetters no longer would be exempt from military service. In mid-June, repeating local gossip, Jones's diary read:

Grant has *used up* nearly a hundred thousand men—to what purpose? We are not injured, after withstanding this blow of the concentrated power of the enemy. It is true some bridges are burned, some railroads have been cut, and the crops in the line of the enemy's march have been ruined; but our army is intact: Lee's losses altogether, in killed and wounded, not exceeding a few thousand.[13]

It was too early yet for Jones to realize that the Confederacy was nearing a point beyond which no nation can survive. Lee gleaned this truth quite clearly at times and then quickly pushed it out of his mind. So, too, did most members of Davis's Cabinet; and even the President himself, although busy with beating down political antagonists and second-guessing his generals, may have read correctly the writing on the wall. In any event he realized that a route of escape must be opened. While army trains hauled supplies by wagon from the disruption of the Richmond & Petersburg Railroad (using a long way round via Dinwiddie Court House, a distance of approximately thirty miles), Negro laborers were employed with fine results in repairing the Richmond & Danville. Just twenty-three days after Kautz had been at Burkeville the line looked in splendid condition.[14]

If one did not partake in these railroad raids, life in camp before Petersburg became a thorough bore in the intervals between mail calls, as Wash Roebling could attest. Wash's delight was a full-grown slave boy, called Jeff Davis, who thought there were 1,400 days in a year and that he was, as a result, little more than a mere child.

"Did you ever hear of God?" Wash asked.

"Do him lib down on de Blackwater?" "Jeff Davis" countered.

Except for the sport of twitting slaves, there was little enough amusement before Petersburg. Jeff was taught to eat flies as fast as Wash and his friends could catch them. The "elephant beetle," which could carry an object as large as a handbag of tobacco on its back, became a very valuable discovery; novels like *Vanity Fair* were reread in those periods when the Federal "siege progresses with horrible slowness"; and Wash, commenting that General Custer's female "servant?" had been driven from camp, wondered if Meade's next meddling would be "forbidding correspondence more than twice a week with one's sweetheart." Solitaire ran out as a favorite card game and cribbage took its place. When given a copy by a picket, Wash laughed at the *Petersburg Express*, noting that "it is a dirty little sheet not as large as a theatre handbill, and is a foot long by 6 inches wide." A camp artist drew pictures for Wash's sweetheart, Emily Warren, to enjoy.[15]

But events were soon to quicken. And many would wonder how, considering his keen military intelligence, Grant could at times seem to lack common sense.

No one ever would pin a medal on Meade as a superior tactician, yet from the start he labeled the proposal of Lieutenant Colonel Henry Pleasants of the 48th Pennsylvania Infantry "all clap-trap and nonsense." Pleasants, an engineer before the war, noticed "a little cup of a ravine near to the enemy's works" at Petersburg that he felt could be successfully mined. Two lateral galleries, carefully ventilated, would have to be excavated for a distance of over five hundred yards, but Pleasants so thoroughly convinced Burnside of the feasibility of his scheme that the General sanctioned it. The digging began on June 25 and continued through the lazy, lethargic days until July 23, providing Grant with the lame excuse that he had allowed the project to be pursued since it gave his men something to occupy their interest.

When at last the galleries were completed, they were packed with 8,000 pounds of powder. After the explosion, Burnside's IX Corps was expected to occupy Cemetery Hill, an elevation four hundred yards away. The V and XVIII Corps were to follow, fan out, and establish positions leading to the capitulation of Petersburg and Richmond.

The explosion was set for 3:30 P.M. on July 30. Burnside selected a division of colored troops who had never been in battle to lead the charge, but Meade rectified this blunder by ordering seasoned white divisions to precede the Negroes. General James H. Ledlie, new and untested in the Army of the Potomac, was assigned command of the assault on Cemetery Hill.

A defective splice caused the fuse to fizzle out, and an hour passed before it could be repaired and relighted. Suddenly the ground rumbled and shook as though caught in an earthquake. A mass of earth, shaped like an inverted cone, rose two hundred feet. Forked tongues of flame darted through this earthen upheaval. "The mass," Horace Porter reported, "seemed to be suspended for an instant in the heavens; then there descended great blocks of clay, rock, sand, timber, guns, carriages, and men whose bodies exhibited every form of mutilation."

As the dust cleared away, the troops stared at a frightful scene. Before them yawned a crater 30 feet deep, 60 feet wide, and 170 feet long. In its debris men were buried up to their necks, others to their waists, still others with only their legs and arms protruding. To add to this hellishness came the roar of 110 Federal cannon and 50 mortars. Rebels and Yankees clambered into the crater only to discover the sides were so steep that once in they could not escape. Disorganized men met, "tumbling aimlessly about" amid the dead and dying. Union General Stephen M. Weld, Jr., remembered, "I could not raise my hands." The Northern commander, Ledlie, was nowhere to be seen; he was in the rear, cowering in a "bomb-proof," or shelter, "soliciting and obtaining whiskey to stimulate his courage." [16]

Ledlie's disgusted staff member, Major William H. Powell, described what the men experienced:

The whole scene of the explosion struck every one dumb with astonishment as we arrived at the crest of the debris. It was impossible for the troops of the Second Brigade to move forward in line, as they had advanced; and, owing to the broken state they were in, every man crowding up to look into the hole, and being pressed by the First Brigade, which was immediately in rear, it was equally impossible to move by the flank, by any command, around the crater. Before the brigade commanders could realize the situation, the two brigades became inextricably mixed, in the desire to look into the hole.

However, Colonel [Elisha G.] Marshall yelled to the Second Brigade to move forward, and the men did so, jumping, sliding, and tumbling into the hole, over the debris of material, and dead and dying men, and huge blocks of solid clay. . . . A partial formation was made by General [William F.] Bartlett and Colonel Marshall with some of their troops, but owing to the precipitous walls the men could find no footing except by facing inward, digging their heels into the earth, and throwing their backs against the side of the crater, or squatting in a half-sitting, half-standing posture, and some of the men were shot even there by the fire from the enemy in the traverses. It was at this juncture that Colonel Marshall requested me to go to General Ledlie and explain the condition of affairs. . . .[17]

The spirit of the occasion was impressed upon Grant's aide, Horace Porter, when he heard a sergeant with his leg shot off call to an advancing regiment of colored troops, "Now go in with a will, boys. There's enough of you to eat 'em all up."

"Dat may be all so, boss," a colored sergeant replied, "but the fac' is, we hab n't got jis de bes' kind of appetite for 'em dis mornin'." [18]

By the time the fighting at the crater ended, Grant had added another 4,000 losses to the Union's casualty lists.

Unexpected disasters like the slaughter in the crater led Robert McAllister to send home a copy of the *Army & Navy Journal* bearing an article on "Claims of Widows and Orphans." McAllister added, "You can see how to get your pension, if I am killed or die, without your being fleeced out of half of it." [19]

When it came to the sheerest military absurdity, General Benjamin F. Butler easily ran off with the honors. One way of lifting the siege of Petersburg, Butler proposed, was to secure a gun that would shoot seven miles and, taking direction by compass, burn the city of Richmond with shells of Greek fire. "If that wouldn't do," Colonel Theodore Lyman said, "he had an augur to bore a tunnel five feet in diameter, and he was going to bore to Richmond and suddenly pop up in somebody's basement while the family were at breakfast!" [20]

Grant had far more pressing matters to which he must attend immediately (or "immeejetly," as the General invariably pronounced that word). Sheridan replaced Hunter as commander in the Valley and was supported by the divisions of Wilson and Torbert, whose cavalrymen were part of the pride of the Army of the Potomac. In essence, Grant told Sheridan either "to follow Early to the death" or at least gain final "possession of the Virginia Central." Early withdrew to Fisher's Hill, located near Strasburg on the now-useless Manassas Gap Railroad. Here Early was reinforced by Joseph B. Kershaw's infantry division and Fitz Lee's cavalry. General George T. Anderson transported his division by rail to Culpeper, where he could protect Early's flank and threaten Sheridan's rear.

Little Phil, however, acutely aware of the approaching elections, determined to create no new causes for alarm among the rabid anti-Lincoln factions. Sheridan's advance stopped at Berryville, six miles northeast of Winchester; then, when Early reoccupied Winchester and Martinsburg on August 17, Sheridan discreetly withdrew to Harper's Ferry, where he could harvest the crops and further disrupt the Baltimore & Ohio Railroad. Since Early remained in the lower Valley, Sheridan occupied Charlestown on August 28 and Berryville on September 3. Under no circumstances did he wish a head-on engagement, for if he were defeated, both Maryland and Pennsylvania would be reopened to Early's raiders.

Grant sent Warren's V Corps once more to bedevil the Richmond & Petersburg Railroad so that Lee must withdraw forces from Early to keep the Petersburg, a principal supply route, from being permanently cut off. On August 18 Warren arrived at Globe Tavern. The IX Corps strengthened him. Three days of Confederate attacks were driven off. Hancock's II Corps were at Ream's Station on August 22, happily tearing up an additional seven miles of track. Lee threw nine brigades of A. P. Hill's III Corps and Hampton's cavalry against Hancock. The new recruits under Hancock did not fight any better than other hastily trained soldiers; but although Hancock was severely battered and five of his fieldpieces captured, the action changed nothing.[21]

The loss of the Petersburg was like cutting off a leg to Lee. He was without corn, and another crop would not mature locally until late September. President Davis and Secretary Seddon sympathized almost pathetically. Georgia, the supply source on which they had depended in emergencies, was littered with rail lines destroyed by Sherman. Local sources of corn in Virginia, Seddon warned, had done very poorly.

Grant, likewise concerned over supplies, asked Major E. L. Wentz of the United States Military Railroads to construct a line from City Point to Globe Tavern. Wentz was a good-humored, inventive fellow. Materials from the defunct Norfolk & Petersburg and the Richmond & York River railroads suited his purpose; other equipment was imported from Alexandria; and in just a shade over two weeks Wentz presented Grant with his military railroad.[22]

The heat and dust which made the first weeks of the investment so hard on the men of the exhausted Army of the Potomac finally wore away. Even Douglas Freeman admitted that after a summer of reverses Confederate morale sagged. "The stimulus of victory . . . no longer could be applied. . . . There was no great battle any day but a small battle every day, the contest of the sharpshooters, of the mortar companies and of the other artillerists." [23] What finally knocked the starch out of the Confederates was a coordinated action that Grant launched in late September. On the south side of the James, Warren advanced along the Boydton (Boydtown) Plank Road, captured Rebel entrenchments at Peebles Farm, and rapidly linked these to Federal works on the Weldon Railroad.

By far the greater triumph came after the Federals had crossed the James at Dutch Gap and demonstrated that even against strong field fortifications "well led troops could still carry out successful frontal attacks." [24] West Point-trained General Edward Ord, who had fought Seminoles before whipping Confederates in various western actions, led the attack on six-sided Fort Harrison. Each wall of this formidable redoubt measured 1,463 feet. Ord advanced in the dark. His forces were divided into two columns each of about 1,000 men. Caps were removed, bayonets fixed. When men, ordered to charge at the double-quick, cried that the distance was too far, Ord sent forward his whole staff to bolster their courage. The roar of the enemy's artillery seemed ceaseless. Many Federals, killed or wounded, sank to the ground. The lines paused and a colonel cried, "Come, boys, we must capture this fort—now get up and start."

The colonel's command had an electric effect. The Federals rushed the ditch. Ord saw them scrambling up the parapet and entering the fort. Fifteen guns and several hundred prisoners were captured. Unfortunately Ord was severely wounded in the leg and his command passed to General William Birney, an Alabama Abolitionist who led a body of colored troops. Birney and his soldiers struck the Confederate entrenchments on the New Market Road and quickly overran them.

In the great confusion Grant discovered an unusual invader on the field—his six-year-old son, Jesse, who was dressed in kilts and rode "Little Reb," a black Shetland pony. Porter wrote that "shots were striking the earth and stirring up the dust in every direction." Grant ordered an aide to lead the boy to safety. Jesse put up a terrific argument before he could be persuaded to retire; he was mortified to think he might be branded a coward for leaving the field in the face of danger.[25]

Later, although the Confederates continued to shell Fort

Harrison, Grant looked toward Richmond, only six miles distant. He could recognize the city's church spires.

Phil Sheridan was back in the Shenandoah Valley in mid-October, and camped his cavalrymen at Cedar Grove on the northern end of Massanutten Mountain, Virginia, whose slopes were reputedly impassable. On the 17th Sheridan rode into Washington for a lengthy conference with Halleck and the over-energetic Stanton. Feet paced the War Department floor—Stanton's feet, mostly. Sheridan returned with leisure to his army, spending on October 18 an extra evening in Winchester (for reasons, truly, that only Sheridan could have explained).

Meanwhile, atop Massanutten Mountain, the Confederate officers of General Jubal Early had looked through the moonlight at Cedar Grove. Sleeping men, campfires, pickets stretched out in a peaceful line. Before daybreak on October 19—under a waning moon, the Valley lay cold and still—Early's men came down through a predawn fog.

Fourteen miles away, Sheridan still slept when Early's forces smashed the Union's left flank at Cedar Grove. At eight o'clock the fog lingered, convincing the Union men that under the circumstances they were defeated. An orderly, awakening Sheridan at Winchester at six o'clock that morning, could not say that the firing was continuous. The musketry was that of a Union brigade on reconnaissance, Sheridan decided, rolling over and trying to resume his sleep. But there was no further slumber for Sheridan; awake, breakfasted, he rode off on Rienzi, a powerful and beautiful black horse given to Sheridan by a colonel of the 2d Michigan Cavalry in honor of Sheridan's victory over Jeb Stuart at Yellow Tavern.

Rienzi's sides were sweating when Sheridan, riding hard toward his retreating columns, gave a barking yell of command they all understood.

"Men, by God, we'll whip them yet! We'll sleep in our old camp tonight!"

An officer, who tried to interrupt, received a dressing down from Sheridan.

"Damn you, don't yell at me!"

Sheridan's troops accomplished precisely what he said they would. Jubal Early could offer only one explanation.

"This was the case of a glorious victory given up by my own troops after they had won it, and it is to be accounted for on the ground of the partial disorganization caused by the plunder of the enemy's camps, and from the fact that the men undertook to judge for themselves when it was proper to retire."

Sheridan had captured forty-three pieces of artillery. He was in an exuberant mood. No wonder poets rose to sing the glory of Sheridan—and his horse Rienzi—at Winchester:

> "Hurrah! hurrah for Sheridan!
> Hurrah! hurrah for horse and man!"

Twenty days later the American people went to the polls to select a President.[26]

XIV

Lincoln in Command

Stanton found Lincoln a "damnable" man. Under ideal circumstances an election night would have frayed the nerves of the Secretary of War, but a rain and wind storm this November 8, 1864, had caused irksome delays in telegraphic communications. The President, in such intervals, amused his friends by reading the humorous writings of Petroleum V. Nasby. Stanton believed Lincoln's performance almost blasphemy at a time when the leadership of the nation hung in the balance. "A man has not time to spend half his life in quarrels," Lincoln said, although at the moment he was not identifying a basic difference between Stanton and himself.

The day had been one of assorted amusements. Young Tad with his pet turkey, Jack, had watched the soldiers voting at a poll down on the riverfront.

"Does he vote?" Lincoln asked, nodding at the turkey.

"No," Tad snapped, bristling with his own "election day" nerves. "He is not of age."

Leslie's Weekly predicted that McClellan was the "undoubted favorite." The sportsman-banker, August Belmont, the chairman of the National Democratic Committee, was challenged and turned away from the polls because he had placed two bets on the election, each for $10,000. One wager contended that, if Lincoln won, the war would continue through his second term; the other claimed the war would close before McClellan's first term ended.

At about seven o'clock that evening Lincoln and his "official family" braved the windy downpour to dash to the War Department's telegraphic office for the election returns. Colonel John W. Forney wired from Philadelphia that the President had carried the city by 10,000.

"Forney is a little excitable," Lincoln said.

A rapturous report from Baltimore followed: "15,000 in the city, 5,000 in the State. All Hail, Free Maryland!"

A Boston report that two Unionists had rolled up majorities of 4,000, Lincoln could not believe. The figure must be 400. No, came back the reply, 4,000 was correct; and Congressman Alexander H. Rice explained why: "The Almighty must have stuffed the ballot-boxes."

The mood in the War Department grew cheerier as other results clacked from the telegraph keys. New York for Lincoln by 10,000— now *that* was unbelievable! But the figure stood up.[1] Noah Brooks watched the President "dishing out the oysters" when toward midnight his re-election no longer could be doubted. His majority grew to more than 400,000 as he carried every state except Kentucky, Delaware, and New Jersey and piled up a plurality in the electoral college vote of 212 to 21.

"Mrs. Lincoln will want to know," he said, leaving the War Department sometime after one o'clock.

The rain had stopped.

Two days later, responding to a serenade on the White House lawn, Lincoln answered the question of why the election was necessary:

We can not have free government without elections; and if the rebellion could force us to forego, or postpone a national election, it might fairly claim to have already conquered and ruined us. The strife of the election is but human nature practically applied to the facts of the case. What has occurred in this case, must ever recur in similar cases. Human-nature will not change. In any future great national trial, compared with the men of this, we shall have as weak, and as strong; as silly as wise; as bad and good. Let us, therefore, study the incidents of this, as philosophy to learn wisdom from, and none of them as wrongs to be revenged.

The election, Lincoln said, had "demonstrated that a people's government can sustain a national election, in the midst of a great civil war"—a possibility the world hitherto had not known. The election, the President continued, had demonstrated much more:

It shows also how *sound*, and how *strong* we still are. It shows that, even among candidates of the same party, he who is most devoted to the Union, and most opposed to treason, can receive most of the people's votes. It shows also, to the extent yet known, that we have more men now, than we had when the war began. Gold is good in its place; but living, brave, patriotic men, are better than gold.[2]

The significance of the election lingered in Lincoln's mind as through the remainder of November he worked on his State of the Union message. The states that had voted four years ago, added to the 33,762 votes in the new states of Kansas and Nevada, increased the aggregate vote by 145,551. In addition there were 90,000 military men unable to meet the requirement of returning home to cast their ballots; and the population of the territories had at least tripled. On December 6 the President told Congress why the integrity of the Union never had been more forcibly maintained:

The extraordinary calmness and good order with which the millions of voters met and mingled at the polls, give strong assurance of this [public integrity]. Not only all those who supported the Union ticket, so-called, but a great majority of the opposing party also, may be fairly claimed to entertain, and to be actuated by, the same purpose. It is an unanswerable argument to this effect, that no candidate for any office whatever, high or low, has ventured to seek votes on the avowal that he was for giving up the Union. . . . In affording the people the fair opportunity of showing, one to another and to the world, this firmness and unanimity of purpose, the election has been of vast value to the national cause.

The public debt as of July 1, Lincoln admitted, was $1,740,690,-489.49, and if the war continued for another year $500,000,000 must be added to this sum. He asked Congress that "a limited amount of some future issue of public securities might be held by any bona fide purchaser exempt from taxation, and from seizure for debt," adding, "The great advantage of citizens being creditors as well as debtors, with relation to the public debt, is obvious."

He asked Congress to furnish Liberia with a gunboat "at moderate cost," since "in Liberian hands it would be far more effective in arresting the African slave trade than a squadron in our own hands."

Lincoln warned Congress that he intended to throw his support behind the Thirteenth Amendment, freeing all slaves, which last session had passed the Senate but failed to receive the necessary two-thirds vote in the House. Once Negroes were freed by the Emancipation Proclamation or by any act of Congress, Lincoln warned, "If the people should, by whatever mode or means, make it an Executive duty to re-enslave such persons, another, and not I, must be their instrument to perform it."

The President thanked Almighty God for the "blessings of health and abundant harvests" that graced the Union. No matter where he looked—to affairs with other nations, to conditions within the country—future prospects were bright. Our national telegraph was being connected with Russia across Bering Strait and by Atlantic cable with Great Britain, so that a system of rapid international communication would soon exist. The construction of a national railroad had been started. Mineral resources of incalculable value had been discovered in the territories. Immigration increased, although the laws called for remedies "to prevent the practice of frauds against the immigrants while on their way and on their arrival in the ports." Idaho and Montana should quickly fulfill the requirements for admission as states. The Agricultural Department, which Lincoln had introduced, had become "peculiarly the people's department, in which they feel more directly concerned than in any other." The President concluded:

"In stating a single condition of peace, I mean simply to say that the war will cease on the part of the government, whenever it shall have ceased on the part of those who began it." [3]

Lincoln agreed with Grant that there was a point where further argument with William Tecumseh Sherman became useless, an opinion that implied as much respect as criticism. Among Union generals, Sherman excelled in learning from the present war. In weaponry, for example, he not only recognized the virtue in offense of machine guns, the breach-loading rifle, the rifled cannon, balloons for aerial reconnaissance, iron-plated warships, and deadlier types of the pug-nosed howitzer, but also glimpsed how future wars would employ armored vehicles, incendiary bombs, flamethrowers, and submarines. Contrary to Jefferson Davis, Sherman admired Joseph E. Johnston and laughed off Hood. As much as any howling savage of the jungle or modern advocate of the atom bomb, Sherman understood terror as an instrument of war and peace.

Sherman evolved his own plan for carrying on the war in the South after the fall of Atlanta. He proposed to divide his army, sending one wing to deal with Hood and the Army of Tennessee and marching the other wing to the sea to destroy the South's capacity for supporting the war. As Hood's adversary Sherman selected Virginia-born General George H. Thomas, already feted as "The Rock of Chickamauga." Thomas was a plodder, as perhaps became his two hundred pounds; he was also studious, deliberate, and fastidious—all traits that agitated the impatient Grant. But in time, which was almost always the way with Thomas, he did his work efficiently, and a new stanza to "The Yellow Rose of Texas" celebrated Thomas's victory:

> But the gallant Hood of Texas
> Sure raised hell in Tennessee.

Meanwhile, with the flames of Atlanta for a backdrop, Sherman and his "Bummers" set off "to make all Georgia howl" by beginning their march to the sea in November. Such militia and cavalry that the Confederacy could muster were an annoyance but never a threat to Sherman. Railroad rails were heated and bent into U shapes around the trunks of trees. Plantations were pillaged and often burned. Frequently slaves told the Federals where the family silverware was buried. Sherman was enjoying immensely this "wild adventure of a crazy fool." For six weeks secrecy surrounded his movements. Grant, embarrassed, told visitors to headquarters, "Sherman's army is now somewhat in the condition of a ground-mole when he disappears under a lawn. You can here and there trace his track, but you are not quite certain where he will come out till you see his head." The *London Times* declared that "military history has recorded no stranger marvel than the mysterious expedition of General Sherman, on an unknown route against an undiscoverable enemy." But then Sherman emerged and telegraphed Lincoln, "I beg to present you as a Christmas gift the city of Savannah.'"

True to the promise in the State of the Union message, Lincoln turned to the Thirteenth Amendment, which gave freedom to all slaves. Thurlow Weed of New York, who once had believed he was the supreme wheeler-dealer of the Republican Party, was now willing to yield this title to Abraham Lincoln. "Honest Old Abe" was as honest as necessity required; he would yield to political muscle if by so doing a principle could be gained. With the admission of Nevada, Lincoln faced the requirement of gaining three votes in the House if he was to tip the delicate balance to win political victory for his amendment.

Lincoln sought out Stanton's assistant, Charles A. Dana, who once had been an assistant editor of Horace Greeley's *New York Herald.* Three votes were doubtful—one from New Jersey and two from New York.

"It is a question of three votes or new armies," Lincoln told Dana.

Stanton's assistant believed that those three votes might well be worth "at least a million men." He could not resist Lincoln—not this man who would raise "an intellectual army that would tend to paralyze the enemy and break the continuity of his ideas." Dana enumerated the traits that placed Lincoln above all around him:

> The great quality of his appearance was benevolence and benignity: the wish to do somebody good if he could; and yet there was no flabby philanthropy about Abraham Lincoln. He was all solid, hard, keen intelligence combined with goodness. . . . You felt that here was a man who saw through things, who understood, and you respected him accordingly.[4]

There were, however, desperate doubts lingering when the vote was called in the House. Two men from Missouri were undecided. Dana could not guarantee the New Jerseyman; he was an alternate who might never get a chance to vote. Finally, in the case of the Jerseyman and the two New Yorkers, Dana posed the critical question.

"Well, sir, what shall I say to these gentlemen?"

"I don't know," Lincoln said. "Whatever promise you make to them I will perform." [5]

The vote was called on the last day in January, 1865. *Harper's Weekly* devoted two pages to a pen-and-ink sketch of that memorable scene. Ladies in fine dresses occupied the boxes around the main floor, and many held seats usually reserved for the press. No desk was unattended, no aisle unfilled. Whiskers and bowler hats dominated the sketch. Speaker Schuyler Colfax of Indiana banged his gavel for attention.

"Up to noon," said a contemporary report, "the pro-slavery party are said to have been confident of defeating the amendment, and, after a time had passed, one of the most earnest advocates of the measure said, ' 'Tis the toss of a copper.' " [6]

Pleas for amendments or substitutes had been gaveled down by four o'clock. Now the real voting began. The sentiment of the gallery was loudly, almost boisterously for passage of the amendment. Every "Aye!" brought a shrill cheer of approval. Members of the Cabinet—William Pitt Fessenden, William Dennison, Montgomery Blair—and four Associate Justices of the Supreme Court clung to the back of the seats before them as though entranced. The final passage of the measure was like a fuse lighting a barrel of gunpowder. Outside the Capitol a hundred cannon fired a salute. As far off as Georgetown church bells began to toll.

XV

★ ═══════════════

With Malice Toward None

For Jefferson Davis the last session of the Confederate Congress was no more irritating than many that had preceded it. From the outbreak of hostilities the Southern politicians, in their overwhelming distrust of a strong centralized government, had declined to create a supreme court that might aid the President in ruling on the constitutionality of legislative actions. Richmond's Mechanics Hall was far too cramped to serve the needs of the government. Too hot in summer and too cold in winter, the discomfitures of the building were magnified by an obsession for secret meetings behind locked doors.

By the winter of 1865 shrewd political minds, of which there were many in the Confederacy, understood the high cost of ever having shifted their arena from Washington to Richmond. More than one muttered that the South would have been better off if this damnable war had never started. "Why is it," Lee asked, "that 200,000 men of one blood and one tongue, believing as one man in the fatherhood of God and the universal brotherhood of man, should in the nineteenth century of the Christian era be thus armed with all the appliances of modern warfare and seeking one another's lives? We could settle our differences by compromising and all be at home in ten days." [1]

It was not alone the casualties of the battlefield that distressed Confederate legislators. With equal agony they understood the disastrous losses they suffered in the Federal Congress. No longer was there a stanch Democrat in the White House to veto the legislation that most alarmed the South. In large measure the voice of Southern opposition had been turned into stone. As a result the national railroad would follow the route of the Union Pacific instead of the Southern course so vigorously expounded by Dixie Democrats. As a result the once-vetoed Homestead Act, which tied people to the central government through a personal subsidy, was now the law of the North. As a result the innovations of Justin S. Morrill of Vermont, creating the resources for a university in every state, were now in ascendancy. Added to the abolition of slavery, Lincoln had tanned their hides.

Why were there those in Richmond ready to blame every setback on Jefferson Davis? Whether the defeat was on the battlefield or in the halls of Congress, Davis always was called to account. Why? Was this one of the traditions belonging to the office of the Confederate presidency? The South, as a one-crop agricultural society dependent on cotton that it could not eat, could turn on Davis for predicting that Lincoln's threatened naval blockade would never work. Too late, Jefferson Davis, holding back the shipment of cotton for a higher price, learned the miserable truth: Yankee shipbuilders had produced enough ships to make Lincoln's blockade effective. In consequence an increasing number of Southerners, hungry and saddled by inflation and a domestic debt that the South could not pay in five generations, said, with sarcasm, "Thank you, President Davis."

A touching tale is told of an afternoon visit that winter paid by General Lee to the Richmond home of Varina Davis, where he was served *café au lait* in a fine Sèvres cup. The General smiled. "My cups in camp are thicker, but this is thinner than the coffee," he told the President's wife.

The winter of 1865 was cold and miserable and made Lee appear all the nobler for his outward cheer. Daily he visited his soldiers in their trenches. He was filled with the homely sayings of a frontier lay preacher: "Do your duty" and "Human virtue should be equal to human calamity." Watching him all day in the saddle, John Esten Cooke, an author who served in the Confederate ranks, believed "he seemed to be made of iron."

The reality of Confederate life could not be escaped. Its Treasury notes sold at less than two cents on the dollar. Its Congress, debating whether the Negro should be taken into the army, a measure that Lee approved, did not consent until March, 1865, and then without any promise of eventual emancipation. At nightfall the bolder of the young Confederates sneaked into Petersburg to dance with the girls.

In the late fall and early winter of 1864–65 the fighting at Petersburg was practically at a standstill. "Put no reliance in what I can do individually," Lee warned Jefferson Davis, "for I believe that will be very little." The shortages of food became unimaginable.

March 4, 1865, began as a dark and gloomy day in Washington. As Lincoln placed his hand on the Bible to take the oath of office, sunlight burst through the clouds and spectators remarked that the coincidence was an omen of coming good fortune. The sunbeams were like golden streams on which Lincoln hung the bejeweled words of his Second Inaugural: "With malice toward none; with charity toward all. . . ." Lincoln wrote Thurlow Weed, "I expect [the Second Inaugural] to wear as well as—perhaps better than—any thing I have produced," yet he did not expect it to be immediately popular. "Men are not flattered by being shown there has been a difference of purpose between the Almighty and them." [2]

Lincoln's lined face revealed the deepening impact of the war's strain. There were frequent recurrences of illness, and one Cabinet meeting was held in his bedroom. He was determined to leave no possibility unexplored. Thus in early February he had met on a boat off Fortress Monroe with three Confederate agents to negotiate, in Davis's reported words, "to secure peace to the two countries." The choice of words doomed the conference before it started; the only way peace could be secured, Lincoln had replied, was on the basis of "the people of our one common country." But Davis was still convinced that the Confederacy could win its independence and accused Lincoln of "bad faith."

On March 28—the day the Confederate Congress recessed—Lincoln held his first and only meeting with his two architects of military victory, Sherman and Grant. The place was the cabin of the steamer *River Queen*, again anchored off Fortress Monroe. Admiral David Porter accompanied the two generals in the rowboat that brought them to the President. The usual amenities were exchanged. Sherman amused the President with humorous incidents of the march to the sea and denied anew that he bore any personal responsibility for the shameful burning of Columbia, South Carolina. Lincoln wondered why Sherman had enjoyed the ease of mind to leave his army in Goldsboro, North Carolina. Recently he had been joined by the troops of two excellent generals, John M. Schofield and Alfred H. Terry, and either gentleman, Sherman replied, could handle any situation that might develop. The conference turned to ending the war. Time and again Lincoln asked the same questions: "Must more blood be shed? Cannot this last bloody battle be avoided?" [3]

Sherman described the scene in the cabin of the *River Queen* as Lincoln pleaded for hostilities to cease. After the perspective of seven years, Sherman wrote:

I ought not and must not attempt to recall the words of that conversation. Of course none of us then foresaw the tragic end of the principal figure of that group, so near at hand; and none of us saw the exact manner in which the war would close; but I know that I felt, and believe the others did, that the end of the war was near. The imminent danger was that Lee, seeing the meshes closing surely around him, would not remain passive; but would make one more desperate effort; and General Grant was providing for it, by getting General Sheridan's cavalry well to his left flank, so as to watch the first symptoms, and to bring the Rebel army to bay till the infantry could come up.

Meanwhile I only asked two weeks stay—the "status quo"—when we would have our wagons loaded, and would start from Goldsboro for Burkesville via Raleigh. Though I can not attempt to recall the words spoken by any one of the persons present on that occasion, I know we talked generally about what was to be done when Lee's & Johnston's armies were beaten and dispersed. On this point Mr. Lincoln was very full. He said that he had long thought of it, that he hoped the end could be reached without more bloodshed, but in any event, he wanted us to get the deluded men of the Rebel armies disarmed and back to their homes, that he contemplated no revenge—no harsh measures, but quite the contrary, and that their suffering and hardships in the war, would make them the more submissive to Law. I cannot say that Mr. Lincoln or anybody else used this language at the time but I know I left his presence with the conviction that he had in his mind, or that his Cabinet had, some plan of settlement ready for application the moment Lee & Johnston were defeated. . . .[4]

Grant left Lincoln by railroad on the morning of March 29. The President, walking down to the station to bid farewell, impressed Horace Porter as looking "more serious" than ever he had seen him. The rings under his eyes had darkened.

"Good-bye, gentlemen," Lincoln called as the train clanged its bell for departure. "God bless you all! Remember, your success is my success."

The train chugged on. Grant puffed on his cigar, turned to Porter, and said, "I think we can send him some good news in a day or two." [5]

The two factors that had delayed Grant's spring offensive—days of incessant, drenching rain, the absence of Sheridan and his cavalry in the Valley—suddenly disappeared. The roads dried and hardened, permitting the Union to start its push to victory.

Grant moved his columns southwestward toward Dinwiddie Court House on the night of March 29. The Federals, advancing some thirty miles beyond Grant's headquarters at City Point, steadily increased the uneasiness of the Confederates as they were pressed back to the vital Southside Railroad. The fighting grew sharp and desperate. Grant pushed his lines in parallels east and west of the Southside, clearly intending also to cut the Richmond & Danville, which would leave Lee completely without a route of supply.

But Grant was after a more disruptive target in Five Forks, ten miles north of Dinwiddie Court House, where five roads intersected on the edge of a well-watered forest. No matter what the hazard, Lee had warned, Five Forks must be held. General Tom Rosser arrived with a mess of fresh shad. Pickets reported there was not a Yankee within sight. Generals Fitzhugh Lee and George Pickett joined Rosser in this unexpected feast. The Confederate trio was picking the meat from their teeth when Phil Sheridan struck. George Alfred Townsend, a reporter, could hardly credit the rout he witnessed at Five Forks on April 1:

"Imagine along a line of a full mile, thirty thousand men struggling for life and prestige; the woods gathering about them—but yesterday the home of hermit hawks and chipmunks—now ablaze with bursting shells, and showing in the dusk the curl of flames in the tangled grass, and rising up the boles of the pine trees, the scaling, scorching tongues." [6]

Lee's only hope now was to join Joseph E. Johnston, who had been restored to command of the Army of Tennessee and was somewhere in North Carolina. Lee had asked that stores be left him at Amelia Court House, forty miles southwest of Richmond, but when his hungry, gaunt-eyed soldiers arrived at this depot the cupboard was bare. Jefferson Davis later was accused of having appropriated the supplies at Amelia, a charge he indignantly denied.[7] Grant had blocked every route by which Lee could escape from Virginia. Only the lonely ride to Appomattox remained.

On a beautiful Sunday, April 2, Jefferson Davis was at services in St. Paul's Church when a messenger from Lee reached Richmond with the news that Grant had overwhelmed Petersburg.

Confederate troops retreated to Danville, whither the President, assembling the heads of the bureaus in his office, now determined to re-establish the government somewhere deeper in the South.

All manner of horse-drawn vehicles filled the streets as civilians raced to quit threatened Richmond. Captain Clement Sullivane saw "few sleeping eyes during the pandemonium of that night." The scene he beheld was such as "probably the world never has witnessed." Either "incendiaries or (more probably) fragments of bombs from the arsenal" had lighted the city until midnight had been turned into the blazing light of midday:

Three high arched bridges were in flames; beneath them the waters sparkled and dashed and rushed on by the burning city . . . as a magazine exploded, a column of white smoke rose up as high as the eye could reach, instantaneously followed by a deafening sound. The earth seemed to rock and tremble as with the shock of an earthquake, and . . . the rattle as of thousands of musketry would follow, and then all was still for the moment except the dull roar and crackle of the fast-spreading fires. . . .

By daylight on the 3rd a mob of men, women and children, to the number of several thousands, had gathered at the corner of 14th and Cary streets, and other outlets in front of the bridge. . . . The depot doors were forced open and a demoniacal struggle for the countless barrels of hams, bacon, whisky, flour, sugar, coffee, etc. raged about the buildings among the hungry mob. The gutters ran whisky, and it was lapped as it flowed down the streets, while all fought for a share of the plunder. The flames came nearer and nearer, and at last caught in the commissariat itself. . . .[8]

— Those portions of Richmond that escaped destruction owed their existence to the Union troops who entered the city at dawn and extinguished the fires.

Lincoln visited Richmond on April 4. The President was embarrassed by the uproarious welcome of former slaves—"I'd rather see him than Jesus,"[9] one colored woman cried—and accepted with quiet amusement how at the sight of him the ladies of Richmond turned their heads sharply aside or slammed down the blinds to their windows. General Godfrey Weitzel, in charge of the troops of occupation, had established his headquarters in Jefferson Davis's home on Clay Street. Thomas Thatcher Graves, a member of Weitzel's staff, recalled Lincoln's quick interest in the desk in the reception room. "This must have been President Davis's office," he said, and seated himself. Graves described Lincoln, with legs crossed, gazing "far off with a serious, dreamy expression." His thoughts remained a secret. Graves's comment that the housekeeper was not on the premises brought Lincoln from his chair in a bounce.

"Come," he exclaimed, "let's look at the house!"

The youth and the President carefully explored the rooms and Graves saw a "boyish expression" on Lincoln's face. Then Weitzel arrived with a number of Richmond officials, and Lincoln's countenance resumed its grave lines as he conferred with this party behind closed doors. Later, after visiting Libby Prison and Castle Thunder, Weitzel inquired how to deal with these "conquered people." Lincoln replied that he no longer gave orders concerning military affairs; then he told Weitzel, "If I were in your place I'd let 'em up easy, let 'em up easy." [10]

One can only conjecture what must have been the nature of Lincoln's thoughts as he leaned back and crossed his feet atop Jefferson Davis's desk. The full extent of the war, which was fought in ten thousand places, was beyond the comprehension of any man. Its cost in monetary and property loss cannot be calculated. The Union dead numbered 360,222, including 110,000 dying of wounds. The wounded who survived were 275,175. The Confederate dead were estimated at 258,000, including 94,000 who died on the fields of battle. No count was kept of the Rebel wounded, and the Confederacy's total manpower involved in the war likewise was unknown. The Federals in uniform in April, 1865, were probably 1 million of the from 2 to 2.3 million who served at various times during the conflict. Again, the number of Confederates in action can only be guessed, and most authorities accept between 600,000 and 700,000 as a reasonable figure.[11] Practically no official Confederate records exist for the fighting from the Battle of the Wilderness to Lee's surrender at Appomattox.[12]

Few realized that, despite a lack of a West Point education, Lincoln held an advantage over Davis. As a young man Lincoln had lectured on "Discoveries and Inventions" at the Springfield Lyceum; surveying roads and platting towns gave him a fundamental understanding of engineering; he had invented a device for lifting ships over shoals and was recognized as an effective patent lawyer. Unfortunately, hotheaded General James W. Ripley, Chief of Army Ordnance, fought any advance that called for tactical changes, but Lincoln had a friend at West Point, Captain Stephen Vincent Benét (grandfather of the late poet), who tested new military inventions for him. Lincoln personally supervised a secret project to develop an explosive using a chlorate base so that the Union would not be dependent on the importation of niter from India.[13]

Lincoln foresaw that new weaponry alone was changing the nature of war, and it was not inappropriate that his Second Inaugural Ball was held in the Patent Office of the Smithsonian Institution. Among the President's closest friends was Dr. Joseph Henry, the institute's director, and Lincoln also was admired by the correspondent for *Scientific American,* who enjoyed the President's "constant flow of genial mirth." [14] Lincoln talked not only about how war had changed but also of how developments then on the drafting boards would make its future more devastating. Obviously the plans of Dr. Solomon Andrews of Perth Amboy, New Jersey, for a dirigible-type, self-steering airship that could drop bombs on enemy concentrations was never brought to Lincoln's serious investigation. Dr. Andrews's airship worked.

Epilogue

John James Toffey, a New Jersey officer on hospital duty in the capital, went to Ford's Theater on April 14 where Laura Keene was starring in *Our American Cousin*. He was delighted to see President and Mrs. Lincoln in the front box, for this was the kind of amusing incident Toffey liked to include in his letters home. At about ten-fifteen a shot was heard.

I took no notice of it neither did any of the Audience [Toffey wrote], as it was thought to be part of the performance till we saw a man leap from the Presidents Box and light on the stage, he lingered a second and then shot off like an arrow. Every one was struck with astonishment until he had disappeared behind the scenes, when it was announced that the President was shot. . . . I had a Revolver with me, and would to God I had presence of mind enough at the time the man jumped to have shot him. Several other officers had revolvers but the thing was done so quick that there was hardly time to draw them and shoot. . . .[1]

Twenty-five years later, speaking on "The Death of Abraham Lincoln," Walt Whitman said:

The final use of the greatest men of a Nation is not with reference to their deeds in themselves, or their direct bearing on their times or lands. The final use of a heroic-eminent life—especially of a heroic-eminent death—is its indirect filtering into the nation and the race, and to give, often at many removes, but unerringly, color and fibre to the Personalism of the youth and maturity of that age, and all ages, of mankind. Then there is a cement to the whole People, subtler, more underlying than any thing in written Constitution, or courts or armies —namely, the cement of a first-class tragic incident thoroughly identified with that People, at its head, and for its sake. Strange, (is it not?) that battles, martyrs, blood, even assassination, should so condense— perhaps only really, lastingly condense—a Nationality.[2]

In the century that followed, among books in English, only those about Christ would outnumber those about Lincoln.

The orders issued to Lieutenant Colonel Benjamin D. Pritchard, when his Union regiment left Macon, Georgia, on May 7, 1865, revealed the nation's vindictive grief over Lincoln's assassination— "Capture or kill Jefferson Davis,"—this man who, in the judgment of President Andrew Johnson, deserved to hang for crimes "worse than murder." In the damp, chilly dawn of May 10 Pritchard's cavalry found Davis and his party encamped near the small town of Irwinsville, Georgia. Grimly the Confederate President watched as a trooper advanced.

"He leveled his carbine at me," Davis recalled for the *New York Herald*, "but I expected, if he fired, he would miss me, and my intention was in that event to put my hand under his foot, tumble him off on the other side, spring into the saddle, and attempt to escape. My wife . . . ran forward and threw her arms around me. Success depending on instantaneous action, and, recognizing that the opportunity had been lost, I turned back. . . ."

Completely untypical of Lincoln was the blood lust of many who professed to love him. Their behavior toward the Rebel ex-President was savage and verged on the hysterical. Intoned the self-righteous editors of *Harper's Weekly*, "Jefferson Davis must be tried for treason. If convicted he must be sentenced. If sentenced he must be executed." Added the self-righteous editors of the *Chicago Tribune*, "We hold if that most guilty and infamous of men is suffered to escape the penalties he has earned, there is not a murderer, a robber, or a perjurer in all the land and who may not with propriety plead the lenience that was extended to him, as a reason why all punishment should cease, and why stabbing, poisoning, arson and robbery should be considered offences no more. . . ."

The confinement of Davis in a dark casement of Fortress Monroe was in itself wicked, but when he was manacled like a common felon the world expressed its revulsion. Davis bore his plight with a stubborn, stiff-jawed dignity. "It was long before I was permitted to hear from my wife and children," he said, "and this, and things like this, was the power which education added to the savage cruelty." Saner voices eventually were heard in the North, none more emphatic than that of Chief Justice Salmon P. Chase; finally Cornelius Vanderbilt and Horace Greeley posted a bond for $100,000; and in May, 1867, Jefferson Davis once more became a free man.[3]

Sarah Anne Dorsey, a girlhood friend of Varina's, turned over to the Davis family Beauvoir, a house in Biloxi, Mississippi, that faced the coast of the Gulf of Mexico. Jefferson Davis was sixty-nine when he went to Beauvoir, and in its beautiful surroundings he passed the last twelve years of life. The home was such as only a prosperous antebellum plantation owner could build. Slates imported from England covered its roof, its frame was built of cypress cut in Back Bay swamp, its foundation and chimneys were constructed of slave-made bricks, and decorators and carpenters brought from New Orleans accounted for its excellent styling.

East of the veranda stood the cottage studio where for three years Jefferson Davis toiled on *The Rise and Fall of the Confederate Government*. With the help of a servant he erected the bookshelves that lined the walls. To the left of the clock on the mantel hung a portrait of Franklin Pierce, a gift from the President whom Davis had served as Secretary of War; on the right hung a likeness of Senator Jesse Speight, whose death in 1847 created the vacancy in the Senate to which Davis was appointed by the governor of Mississippi. No one appreciated better than Varina his acute sensitivity: "Even a child's disapproval discomposed him." His lip trembled when he set off to work, calling himself "a citizen of no land under the sun."

Jefferson Davis threw himself into long periods of work to forget the hostile world surrounding him. Time meant nothing to him—he would finish his book, for example, at four o'clock in the morning after eight straight hours of dictation.[4] The wholeness of Davis was what gave distinction to his work. No antipathy that he ever had felt, no prejudice that ever had influenced his judgment, was omitted from the pages of *The Rise and Fall of the Confederate Government*. He was almost childlike in being above deceit. In this respect he appealed even to Southern historians, who, using his clichés, found it easy to cast him in a role that simplified all those tragic years from 1861 to 1865. They spoke of the "brothers' war" without conceding that brothers did not fight as viciously or as vindictively as did the soldiers of Grant and Lee in the prolonged struggles that carried them to Cold Harbor and on to Petersburg.

A profound historian, Roy F. Nichols, began to worry. Were many points being missed? What more explicitly did Anglo-American history have to teach us than the fact that "in expanding societies there may on occasion come a time when growth exceeds the capacity to govern"? Were the American Revolution and the Civil War as alike as they seemed? There was no ocean, no benefit of a France or Spain to help one competing partner against the other. Where the British Empire had ruled the colonies, the choice had been "between self-government and continued inferiority as an outpost"; but "the Confederacy, on the other hand, was maneuvering to keep a superiority and power that it had enjoyed and that at heart it preferred to exclusion from the system it had dominated." How deep was the "kinship" between North and South if the South lost the veto and the power to control it provided?

The questions multiply, if not the answers. North and South, by the nature of their individual structure, stumbled into dangerous paradoxes. How radical factions in the North endangered Lincoln's leadership was clearly illustrated by the Union's inability to make more use of the weaponry of the Industrial Age; but the South, in its devotion to *laissez faire*, could not unite and so develop the managerial capacity essential to mobilizing resources and transportation. Why was the South, condemning the "damyankee" and terrorized by the prospect of slave insurrection, willing to give—and to give knowingly—its life to a Lost Cause? Edward A. Pollard, a Richmond editor, understood that the Confederacy had "thrown down the sword to take up the weapons of argument, not indeed under any banner of fanaticism, or to enforce a dogma, but simply to make the honourable conquest of reason and justice." In short, after the South surrendered on the battlefield, it fought "to regain political power." [5]

Jefferson Davis's *The Rise and Fall of the Confederate Government* was intended to add courage to those who must carry on for the South. It apologized for nothing. The war was one of "aggressions"—conceived by Lincoln and his party—to extend their sectional power over the South.

"To conceal their real motive," Davis wrote, "and artfully to appeal to the prejudice of foreigners, they declared that slavery was the cause of the troubles of the country, and of the 'rebellion' which they were engaged in suppressing."

The Constitution gave them no such power, so why had they changed this contract with the states? The inflexible Davis continued, "The answer is, It was wrought by the same process and on the same plea that tyranny has ever employed against liberty and justice—the time-worn excuse of usurpers—necessity; an excuse which is ever assumed as valid, because the usurper claims to be the sole judge of his necessity." [6]

Inflexibility was not part of Lee's character. Generals who believed they must flee to a foreign country since they could not live under the Washington government must follow their impulses; but Lee argued that the South needed its leaders even more desperately now than before and would not join any such movement. He declined emphatically the opportunity to lead bands of bushwhackers in punitive raids against the North. Grant had been a fair and reasonable man in arranging surrender terms, Lee told his troops; tears were too close to the surface to discuss the matter further. He turned his horse toward Richmond, eager to rejoin his wife, family, and friends. People lined the roadside to cheer him, and mothers held aloft young children and babies who were called "Lee" so that in later years they could say that they had glimpsed their noble namesake.

Unusual offers came to Lee. A New York firm set a salary of $50,000 a year if he would promote its trade in the South. An admiring nobleman offered him an estate and an allowance of $15,000 a year if he would settle in England. Lee simply shook his head. There was no price tag that could be placed on his heart or conscience. Wisdom led him "to acquiesce in the result." One Sunday when a Negro walked to the communion table, Lee kept eyebrows from arching when he knelt at the chancel rail not far from the black man.

Lee's dream was of "some little quiet place in the country," but the small farm never materialized. Instead he became president of Washington College, a virtually bankrupt institution in Lexington, Virginia. His salary was $1,500 a year and he earned every penny of it, for he rehabilitated the school. When Jefferson Davis was freed from Fortress Monroe, Lee wrote, "Your release has lifted a load from my heart which I have not words to tell, and my daily prayer to the great Ruler of the world is, that He may shield you from all future harm, guard you from all evil, and give you the peace which the world cannot take away." [7]

Lee at Washington College was still a man who loved homely humor. "Young gentlemen," he told entering students, "we have no printed rules. We have but one rule and it is that every student must be a gentleman." A professor characterized him: "To the faculty he was an elder brother, beloved and revered, and full of tender sympathy." The essence of his philosophy he found in lines by Hafiz, the Mussulman poet:

Learn from your Orient shell to love thy foe,
And store with pearls the hand that brings thee woe;
Free like yon rock, from base vindictive pride,
Emblaze with gems the wrist that rends thy side:
Mark where yon tree rewards the stony shower,
With fruit nectareous, or balmy flower;
All nature cries aloud, shall man do less
Than heal the smiter and the railer bless?

In 1869 Lee began to weaken. He traveled to Georgia and Florida but could not shake an irritating cold. The baths at Hot Springs availed him nothing. On a Sabbath the following September he attended church on a damp, chilly afternoon. He could not say the blessing at dinner. On October 12, 1870, the end was gentle. His last words were:

"Strike the tent." [8]

Grant was the victor to whom the spoils belonged. Unhappily he also was part of one of the most unseemly ages of politics, that "almost godless" era of the Boss Tweeds, the Jim Fisks, the Jay Goulds, when these unscrupulous speculators might charge the taxpayer through dishonest contracts $10,000,000 for a building worth $250,000. Grant, with a heart as unembittered as Lincoln's or Lee's, reached the White House at the worst possible time when political bossism in the North was combined with "carpetbagger" reconstruction in the South. Whether Grant had voted for Lincoln in 1860 he would never say or allow any one to guess; the chances were that he did not, since in 1860 (an opinion he later changed) he did not believe that slavery was an issue justifying a war.

Nominated by the Republicans in 1868, Grant easily won election as President, carrying twenty-eight states (Mississippi, Texas, and Virginia could not vote) and piling up a popular vote of

3,015,071 against a loss of eight states and 2,700,613 Democratic votes. There were many positive results of his administration. The most outstanding was the adoption of the Fifteenth Amendment guaranteeing that "the right of the citizens of the United States to vote shall not be denied or abridged by any state on account of race, color, or previous condition of servitude." He celebrated the completion of the transcontinental railroad, the establishment of Yellowstone National Park, and the admission of Colorado, known as "the Centennial State" because it joined the Union in 1876. But Grant, sorely inexperienced in top-level politics (and woefully inefficient in judging a thief or a liar among his friends), was hurt dreadfully by public exposure. The Senate rejected his attempt to annex Santo Domingo. The "Salary Grab Bill of 1873" and the resultant financial panic of that year were blamed on Grant because it raised the presidential salary from $25,000 to $50,000 a year.

Grant engaged in a world tour, was hailed everywhere as a hero, and hoped as a result to gain the presidential nomination for a third term, but the "Mugwumps," or liberals of his party, defeated this ambition. Innocently he became involved in a banking operation with Ferdinand Ward and others; by 1884 the failure of the firm left Grant penniless.

Bankruptcy and harsh criticism as a virtual swindler Grant could endure; starvation he could not. Finally the government began paying the pension Grant deserved as a retired general. The arrival of the first check at Grant's New York City home on East Sixty-Sixth Street created a festive occasion. Grant never forgot the date: March 31, 1885. He made little rolls of the money, passing them out to his wife and sons.

A sore throat, noticeable after eating a raw peach, was the first indication of the cancer that would kill him. He was shunted around from doctor to doctor, pinching pennies by riding trolleys and asking for transfers. A national sympathy blossomed around him. Medical opinions varied as to the malignancy of his condition. The newspapers treated the case humorously. One headline read, GRANT THINKS THE DOCTORS WILL PULL THROUGH. Another declared, A BAD DAY FOR THE DOCTORS. GENERAL GRANT WATCHING THEM CLOSELY. But Dr. George F. Shardy, an expert microscopist, could not make a lark of Grant's affliction. "General Grant is doomed."

Once more Grant became the unyielding warrior. To provide for his family he would write his *Memoirs*. He worked "with his single-minded intensity," from five to six hours a day, and as each page was completed he turned it over to his son, Fred, and his own military biographer, General Adam Badeau, for criticism. There were rumors that someone was writing the *Memoirs* for him, an accusation Grant stoutly denied. "Every day, every hour, is a week of agony. I am easier when employed."

Grant was able to avoid the humid city heat through the generosity of a devoted friend, Joseph W. Drexel, who loaned him a cottage at Mount McGregor, north of Saratoga Springs, New York. When he reached the point where he could not dictate, he painfully scrawled out the pages by hand. In his rocker, eyes half closed against the sun, he worked on the porch of the cottage at Mount McGregor—a stump of a man with a shawl around his shoulders and a stocking cap on his head.

People from the surrounding country [Hamlin Garland wrote in *McClure's Magazine*] came in procession past the cottage, eager to catch a glimpse of the most renowned man of his time. The railway brought other swarms of curious or sympathetic tourists, and they stole near and gazed silently upon the dying man, and then moved on. He was not annoyed as another might have been by these passing shadows. Once he wrote of them: "To pass my time pleasantly, I should like to talk with them if I could." If they bowed to him he returned their salutes; and once, when a woman passing removed her bonnet, he struggled to his feet and removed his hat in acknowledgement. His favorite seat was a willow chair which stood at the northeast corner of the veranda, and there he sat during the middle hours of each day to enjoy the sun and air; as it grew chill, he returned to his fireside. He listened as courteously to the spokesman of a troop of school children, or to a little girl presenting a bouquet, as to a delegation of leading citizens or foreign journalists.[9]

His *Memoirs,* considered by many a classic because of their sincerity and simplicity, were finished one week before his death on July 23, 1885. Thunder shook the hills around Mount McGregor. Lightning knocked down nine people at the railroad station.

The *Boston Globe* sent its New Orleans correspondent to obtain a statement from Jefferson Davis, if he would give one. Gravely Davis replied, "Though he [Grant] invaded our country, it was with an open hand, and, as far as I know, he abetted neither arson nor pillage, and has since the war, I believe, showed no malignity to Confederates either of the military or civil service. Therefore, instead of seeking to disturb the quiet of his closing hours, I would, if it were in my power, contribute to the peace of his mind and the comfort of his body." [10]

Jefferson Davis died on December 6, 1889. The curtain was closed now on the last act of tragedy, and a new generation approached manhood. As Lincoln had said, "with firmness in the right, as God gives us to see the right," the time was one for binding up the nation's wounds.

Notes

Chapter 1. Dramatis Personae

1. Strode, *Jefferson Davis, Confederate President*, p. 308.
2. The original secession states were South Carolina, Georgia, Florida, Alabama, Mississippi, and Louisiana. Texas was seventh, followed by Arkansas, Virginia, Tennessee, and North Carolina. Although Missouri and Kentucky never left the Union, the Confederacy recognized "provisional governments" from these states, presumably wishing thirteen stars on its flag.
3. Nichols, *Blueprints for Leviathan: American Style*, pp. 164–66.
4. *Ibid.*, p. 168.
5. Unless otherwise noted, the quotations concerning the Confederate President are taken from my Introduction to an abridged paperback edition of Jefferson Davis's *The Rise and Fall of the Confederate Government*, pp. 14–15.
6. Nichols, *Blueprints for Leviathan*, pp. 246 *et seq.*
7. Miers, introduction to *Lincoln Day-by-Day*, I, vii–xiii.
8. Basler, *The Collected Works of Abraham Lincoln*, IV, 432–33 (cited hereafter as *Collected Works*).
9. The authoritative work on the evolution of weapons of modern war at this time is Bruce, *Lincoln and the Tools of War*.
10. Miers, *The Great Rebellion*, pp. 66–67.
11. Morison, *The Oxford History of the American People*, p. 235.
12. Freeman, *R. E. Lee*, I, 14–15.
13. Miers, *The Great Rebellion*, pp. 83–84.

14. Miers, "When in Doubt, Fight," *The Saturday Review Gallery*, pp. 30 *et seq.*

15. Angle and Miers, *Tragic Years*, II, 756–62.

16. Miers, "When in Doubt, Fight," pp. 35, 37.

17. Alexander, "A Conflict of Perceptions: Ulysses S. Grant and the Mormons," p. 30.

18. Longstreet, *From Manassas to Appomattox*, p. 554.

CHAPTER 2. "A JACKASS IN THE ORIGINAL PACKAGE"

1. Brooks, *Washington, D.C., in Lincoln's Time*, pp. 127–29.

2. Sandburg, *Abraham Lincoln: The War Years*, II, 539–40.

3. *Ibid.*, p. 538.

4. Thomas, *Abraham Lincoln*, pp. 372–73.

5. Macartney, *Grant and His Generals*, p. 312.

6. Thomas and Hyman, *Stanton*, p. 296.

7. *Ibid.*, p. 297.

8. Porter, *Campaigning with Grant*, p. 22; Brooks, *Washington, D.C., in Lincoln's Time*, pp. 129–30; Leech, *Reveille in Washington, 1860–1865*, p. 312.

9. F. Grant, "Extracts from an Address. . . ." A signed copy of the typescript is in the Illinois State Library. Hereafter all references to Grant are from sources by Ulysses S. Grant.

10. Porter, *Campaigning with Grant*, p. 18.

11. *Ibid.*, pp. 19–21; Brooks, *Washington in Lincoln's Time*, p. 130; Welles, *Diary*, May 11, 1864.

12. Basler, *Collected Works*, VII, 234–35; Mordell, *Selected Essays by Gideon Welles*, pp. 192, 194; *Atlantic Monthly* Vol. 41 (March 1878), pp. 454 *et seq.*

13. Porter, *Campaigning with Grant*, p. 22.

14. Leech, *Reveille in Washington*, pp. 313–14. Grant was nicknamed "Unconditional Surrender" after Donelson.

15. Dowdey, *The Wartime Papers of R. E. Lee*, 682–83 (hereafter cited as *Wartime Papers*); Freeman, *Lee's Dispatches*, pp. 140 ff.

16. Donald, *Why the North Won the Civil War*, p. 38.

17. Dowdey, *Lee's Last Campaign*, p. 36.

18. Donald, *op. cit.*, p. 43.

19. *Lincoln Day-by-Day*, III, 249.

20. Leech, *Reveille in Washington*, p. 314.

21. Porter, *Campaigning with Grant*, p. 23–24.

22. Mearns, "*Lincoln*," p. 68.

23. Freeman, *R. E. Lee,* III, 264.
24. Mordell, *Selected Essays by Gideon Welles,* pp. 195, 197.
25. Grant, *Personal Memoirs,* p. 363.
26. Mearns, "Lincoln," p. 68; Starr, *Bohemian Brigade,* p. 281.
27. Grant, *Memoirs,* p. 359.
28. *Ibid.,* pp. 364–365.
29. *Ibid.,* p. 366.
30. Dowdey, *Wartime Papers,* p. 669; the order was dated February 7, 1864.
31. Dowdey, *Lee's Last Campaign,* p. 4.
32. Dowdey, *Wartime Papers,* p. 673.
33. Dowdey, *Lee's Last Campaign,* p. 45.
34. Dowdey, *Wartime Papers,* p. 692.
35. *Ibid.,* p. 693.
36. Freeman, *R. E. Lee,* III, 264.
37. Fuller, *The Generalship of Ulysses S. Grant,* p. 239.
38. *Ibid.,* pp. 380–81.

Chapter 3. Lee Leaves the Mountain

1. Robertson, *The Civil War Letters of General Robert McAllister,* p. 403n (cited hereafter as *McAllister Letters*). The full manuscript is in the Rutgers University Library (cited hereafter as RUL), but only items of local New Jersey interest have been omitted from the published volume.
2. Agassiz, *Meade's headquarters 1863–1865: Letters of Theodore Lyman,* pp. 81, 83.
3. *Ibid.,* p. 240.
4. *Roebling Mss.,* RUL.
5. Robertson, *McAllister Letters,* pp. 405, 408.
6. Fuller, *Generalship of Grant,* pp. 213 *et seq.*
7. Once re-elected, Lincoln himself removed Butler.
8. Later Wash was to brand the opening campaign as a "great fizzle" and quote Warren as saying, "My suggestions were received with contumely and scorn that was positively insulting." *Roebling Mss.,* RUL.
9. Swinton, *Campaigns of the Army of the Potomac,* pp. 411–12.
10. *War of the Rebellion: . . . Official Records,* Vol. 60, pp. 1017–18; Fuller, *Generalship of Grant,* pp. 214–15. The chief reports concerning the campaign between Grant and Lee are in Vols. 33 and 36 of the *Official Records* (cited hereafter as OR).

11. Fuller, *Generalship of Grant*, p. 215.

12. OR, 33, p. 1321; Freeman, *Lee's Lieutenants*, III, 342.

13. *Ibid.*, pp. 343–46.

14. Freeman, *R. E. Lee*, III, 266–68.

15. Fuller, *Generalship of Grant*, pp. 228–29; Humphreys, *The Virginia Campaign of '64 and '65*, pp. 11, 9; Badeau, *Military History of Ulysses S. Grant*, II, 113; Swinton, *Army of the Potomac*, p. 429.

16. Humphreys, *Virginia Campaign*, p. 11.

17. Angle and Miers, *Tragic Years*, II, 788–93; Moore, *The Rebellion Record*, XI, 440–41; Sorrel, *Recollections of a Confederate Staff Officer*, pp. 226–27.

18. Robertson, *McAllister Letters*, p. 415.

19. Agassiz, *Meade's Headquarters*, pp. 91–92.

20. Porter, *Campaigning with Grant*, pp. 69–70.

CHAPTER 4. "WHEN LINCOLN KISSED ME"

1. Govan and Livingood, *The Haskell Memoirs*, pp. vi, 63. Although Freeman found Haskell's memoirs "charming," he grumbled over an occasional inaccuracy that the present editors find inconsequential. At death Haskell left three completed manuscripts which have been combined for fuller detail into this volume.

2. OR, 36, Part 1, pp. 487–90.

3. Agassiz, *Meade's Headquarters*, pp. 93–94.

4. Govan and Livingood, *The Haskell Memoirs*, pp. 63–64.

5. Freeman, *Lee's Lieutenants*, III, 358.

6. Govan and Livingood, *The Haskell Memoirs*, pp. 65–66.

7. Sorrel, *Recollections*, pp. 230–31.

8. Agassiz, *Meade's Headquarters*, p. 98.

9. *Ibid.*

10. Moore, *Rebellion Record*, XI, 443.

11. Marbaker, *History of the Eleventh New Jersey Volunteers*, pp. 168–69.

12. *Roebling Mss.*, RUL; in the main these criticisms were addressed to Morris Schaff in 1909, who was preparing an article for the *Atlantic Monthly* on the Wilderness campaign.

13. Thomas and Hyman, *Stanton*, pp. 299–300.

14. Starr, *Bohemian Brigade*, pp. 299–300.

15. *Ibid.*, pp. 300–303; Thomas and Hyman, *Stanton*, p. 300; Strong, *Diary*, III, 442; *Lincoln Day-by-Day*, III, 257; Bates, *Lincoln in the Telegraph Office* . . . , p. 246.

16. Basler, *Collected Works*, VII 332.

CHAPTER 5. "ON TO RICHMOND!"

1. Swinton, *Army of the Potomac*, p. 439.
2. Freeman, *R. E. Lee*, III, 297.
3. Sorrell, *Recollections*, pp. 238–39; Freeman, *Lee's Lieutenants*, III, 374–75.
4. Fuller, *Generalship of Grant*, pp. 238–39.
5. Swinton, *Army of the Potomac*, p. 438.
6. Grant, *Memoirs*, p. 408; OR, 36, Part 1, p. 133.
7. Catton, *This Hallowed Ground*, p. 326.
8. Porter, *Campaigning with Grant*, pp. 78–79.
9. Sheridan, *Memoirs*, I, 365–69.
10. *Ibid.*, pp. 369–71.
11. Cooke, *Wearing of the Gray*, p. 7.
12. Davis, *Jeb Stuart*, p. 384.
13. *Ibid.*, p. 385; Miers, *Ride to War*, p. 197, an annotated edition of Henry R. Pyne, *History of the First New Jersey Cavalry* (Trenton, 1871).
14. Sheridan, *Memoirs*, I, 373; Davis, *Jeb Stuart*, p. 385.
15. Davis, *Jeb Stuart*, p. 386.
16. Miers, *Ride to War*, pp. 196–99.
17. Davis, *Jeb Stuart*, pp. 388–89.
18. Miers, *Ride to War*, pp. 199–200.
19. Sheridan, *Memoirs*, I, 376.
20. Davis, *Jeb Stuart*, pp. 392, 393.
21. Sheridan, *Memoirs*, I, 376.
22. *Ibid.*, pp. 377–78.
23. Davis, *Jeb Stuart*, pp. 397 et seq.
24. McClellan, H. B., *Southern Historical Society Papers*, VII, 107–9; Angle and Miers, *Tragic Years*, II, 805–07.
25. Miers, *Ride to War*, pp. 201–02.

CHAPTER 6. THE BLOODY ANGLE

1. *Lincoln Day-by-Day*, III, 257; Welles, *Diary*, June 3, 1864.
2. Boatner, *Civil War Dictionary*, pp. 784–85; Grant, *Memoirs*, pp. 415–17.
3. Robertson, *McAllister Letters*, p. 417; OR, 36, Part 1, pp. 65,

330, 380–91, 490; Dana, *Recollections of the Civil War*, p. 67. Paul Angle, writing an introduction to a paperback edition of Dana's *Recollections* (New York: Collier Books, 1963, pp. 6–7), pointed out how Miss Tarbell had ghost-written Dana's recollections and admitted that fact in her autobiography, *All in the Day's Work* (New York: Macmillan Co., 1939).

4. Robertson, *McAllister Letters*, p. 417n; OR, 36, Part 1, pp. 65, 330, 490–91.

5. *Ibid.*, p. 491; Boatner, *Civil War Dictionary*, p. 788. Generals Anderson and "Maryland" Steuart were among those captured.

6. Porter, *Campaigning with Grant*, p. 110.

7. Robertson, *McAllister Letters*, pp. 418–19. The letter to Mott was dated January 24, 1882.

8. Porter, *Campaigning with Grant*, pp. 110–11.

9. *Ibid.*, pp. 111–12.

10. *Lincoln Day-by-Day*, p. 258; Nicolay to Bates, May 15, 1864, Ms, Library of Congress; Basler, *Collected Works*, VII, 344; Thomas and Hyman, *Stanton*, pp. 300–01; OR, 36, Part 2, p. 369; Part 3, p. 722.

11. Starr, *Bohemian Brigade*, pp. 315–17; Sandburg, *Abraham Lincoln: The War Years*, III, 53 ff.; Basler, *Collected Works*, VII, 348n–49n. The *Daily News* of 1864 bore no connection with the present paper of that name.

12. Starr, *Bohemian Brigade*, pp. 317–18; *Lincoln Day-by-Day*, III, 259.

13. Thomas and Hyman, *Stanton*, pp. 301–02.

14. Boatner, *Civil War Dictionary*, p. 788; Angle and Miers, *Tragic Years*, II, 808.

15. Freeman, *R. E. Lee*, III, 331.

16. Agassiz, *Meade's Headquarters*, pp. 132–33.

CHAPTER 7. THE SPREADING WEB OF WAR

1. Robertson, *McAllister Letters*, pp. 423, 428.

2. Freeman, *Lee's Lieutenants*, III, 496; OR, 36, Part 3, pp. 814–15; Freeman, *R. E. Lee*, III, 340–42.

3. Grant, *Memoirs*, pp. 427, 428, 429–30.

4. Robertson, *McAllister Letters*, pp. 424, 424n; OR, 36, Part 1, pp. 478, 600–01.

5. Freeman, *Lee's Lieutenants*, III, 497–98.

6. *OR*, 36, Part 1, p. 21.
7. Grant, *Memoirs*, pp. 432–33.
8. *Lincoln Day-by-Day*, III, 260.
9. Leech, *Reveille in Washington*, pp. 322–23.
10. *Ibid.*, p. 324.
11. Adams, *Doctors in Blue*, pp. 70, 97, 102.
12. Leech, *Reveille in Washington*, p. 325.
13. Dowdey, *Lee's Last Campaign*, p. 242.
14. DeLeon, *Four Years in Rebel Capitals*, p. 369.
15. *Ibid.*, pp. 353 ff.
16. Jones, *A Rebel War Clerk's Diary*, pp. 374–77.
17. Dowdey, *Lee's Last Campaign*, pp. 243–44.
18. Jones, *Rebel War Clerk*, pp. 377–83.
19. *Ibid.*, p. 384; *Lincoln Day-by-Day*, III, 260; Dowdey, *Lee's Last Campaign*, p. 267.
20. Dowdey, *Lee's Last Campaign*, p. 269.
21. Lee, Jr., *My Father*, p. 127.
22. Taylor, *Four Years with General Lee*, pp. 133–34; Freeman, *Lee's Lieutenants*, III, 498n.

Chapter 8. Should Lincoln Be Dumped?

1. Angle and Miers, *Tragic Years*, II, 822–23.
2. Thomas and Hyman, *Stanton*, pp. 140–41.
3. McClure, *Lincoln and Men of War Times*, p. 127.
4. Angle and Miers, *Tragic Years*, II, 826–27.
5. *Ibid.*, pp. 828–29.
6. Thomas and Hyman, *Stanton*, pp. 308–9, 311.
7. Sandburg, *Abraham Lincoln: The War Years*, III, 70–71; Angle and Miers, *Tragic Years*, II, 829; McPherson, *Political History* ... p. 412.
8. Nicolay and Hay, *Abraham Lincoln: A History*, IX, 40–41.
9. Thomas and Hyman, *Stanton*, pp. 311–12.

Chapter 9. The Great Battle Impends

1. Grant, *Memoirs*, pp. 433–34; *OR*, 36, Part 3, p. 836.
2. Grant, *Memoirs*, p. 436n.

3. *Ibid.*, p. 436.

4. Dowdey, *Lee's Last Campaign*, p. 268.

5. Grant, *Memoirs*, pp. 436–37. Frequently in Southern sources the name is spelled Haw's Shop.

6. *Ibid.*, p. 437.

7. Robertson, *McAllister Letters*, p. 431; Freeman, *Lee's Lieutenants*, III, 500.

8. Robertson, *McAllister Letters*, pp. 430–31.

9. Grant, *Memoirs*, p. 437.

10. Freeman, *Lee's Lieutenants*, III, 503.

11. Grant, *Memoirs*, p. 437.

12. *Ibid.*, p. 438.

13. Angle and Miers, *Tragic Years*, I, 312–13.

14. Fuller, *Generalship of Grant*, p. 275. Fuller organized the first British tank corps in World War I and was a member of the staff in World War II whose plans devastated the Nazis in their field operations. See his *The Conduct of War, 1789–1961*.

15. Sheridan, *Memoirs*, I, 406–07.

16. *Ibid.*, pp. 407–10; the time may have been ten o'clock.

17. *Ibid.*, pp. 410–11; Freeman, *Lee's Lieutenants*, III, 501 *et seq.*

18. Jones, *Rebel War Clerk*, pp. 384, 387.

19. *Ibid.*, pp. 384–85.

20. Grant, *Memoirs*, pp. 409–10.

21. Porter, *Campaigning with Grant*, pp. 174–75.

22. Robertson, *McAllister Letters*, p. 435.

23. Agassiz, *Meade's Headqurters*, p. 106.

24. Jones, *Rebel War Clerk*, p. 386.

25. Freeman, *Lee's Lieutenants*, III, 507; Fuller, *Generalship of Grant*, p. 276.

26. Robertson, *McAllister Letters*, p. 431.

27. Jones, *Rebel War Clerk*, p. 387.

28. Fuller, *Generalship of Grant*, p. 277.

29. Grant, *Memoirs*, p. 440.

CHAPTER 10. COLD HARBOR—GRANT LOSES PATIENCE

1. Fuller, *Generalship of Grant*, pp. 278 *et seq.*

2. Jones, *Rebel War Clerk*, p. 387.

3. Porter, *Campaigning with Grant*, p. 174.

4. Freeman, *R. E. Lee*, III, 384.

5. Fuller, *Generalship of Grant*, p. 280.

6. Swinton, *Army of the Potomac*, p. 485; Johnson and Buel, *Battles and Leaders of the Civil War*, IV, 217.

7. Freeman, R. E. *Lee*, III, 389.

8. Eisenschiml and Newman, *The Civil War: The American Iliad as Told by Those who Lived It*, I, 580–81.

9. Robertson, *McAllister Letters*, p. 432.

10. Oates, *War Between Union and Confederacy*, pp. 366–67.

11. Grant, *Memoirs*, p. 442.

12. *Ibid.*, pp. 443–44; Freeman, R. E. *Lee*, III, 391; Jones, *Rebel War Clerk*, p. 389.

13. Eisenschiml and Newman, *American Iliad*, I ,580.

14. *Lincoln Day-by-Day*, III, 263.

15. Fuller, *Generalship of Grant*, p. 284.

16. Leech, *Reveille in Washington*, pp. 326–27.

17. Grant, *Memoirs*, p. 445.

CHAPTER 11. COUNTERPUNCH

1. Fuller, *Generalship of Grant*, pp. 286–87.

2. Badeau, *Military History*, II, 346–47.

3. Grant, *Memoirs*, pp. 453–54.

4. *Ibid.*

5. Fuller, *Generalship of Lee*, p. 290.

6. *Ibid.*, p. 289.

7. *Ibid.*, p. 290; Grant, *Memoirs*, pp. 45–51.

8. Fuller, *Generalship of Grant*, p. 293.

9. *Roebling Mss.*, RUL.

10. Thomas and Hyman, *Stanton*, pp. 304–05.

11. *Ibid.*, p. 317.

12. Strode, *Jefferson Davis, Confederate President*, pp. 509–10.

13. Davis, *The Rise and Fall of the Confederate Government*, p. 549.

14. *Ibid.*, p. 555.

CHAPTER 12. WIGWAM BY A LAKE

1. Angle and Miers, *Tragic Years*, II, 868.

2. *Ibid.*, pp. 874–75.

3. *Ibid.*, p. 875.
4. Basler, *Collected Works*, VII, 514.
5. Angle and Miers, *The Living Lincoln*, p. 611.
6. Thomas and Hyman, *Stanton*, p. 324.
7. Angle and Miers, *Tragic Years*, II, 877.
8. Basler, *Collected Works*, VII, 393.
9. *Ibid.*, VII, 533.
10. *Ibid.*, VIII, 11.
11. Thomas and Hyman, *Stanton*, p. 317.

CHAPTER 13. IN THE VALLEY

1. Thomas and Hyman, *Stanton*, pp. 318–19.
2. *Ibid.*, p. 319.
3. Welles, *Diary*, II, 70–71.
4. Early, *War Memoirs*, p. 390.
5. *Ibid.*, p. 391.
6. Welles, *Diary*, II, 72–73.
7. Early, *War Memoirs*, p. 392.
8. Freeman, *Lee's Lieutenants*, III, 586–87.
9. Johnston, *Virginia Railroads*, p. 210; Fuller, *Generalship of Grant*, pp. 299–300.
10. Johnston, *Virginia Railroads*, p. 211.
11. *Ibid.*, pp. 211–13.
12. OR, 40, Part 1, p. 626.
13. Jones, *Rebel War Clerk*, pp. 390, 392.
14. Johnston, *Virginia Railroads in the Civil War*, pp. 213–14.
15. *Roebling Mss.*, RUL.
16. Fuller, *Generalship of Grant*, pp. 303–04; Porter, *Campaigning with Grant*, pp. 258–70.
17. Johnson and Buel, *Battles and Leaders*, IV, 559.
18. Porter, *Campaigning with Grant*, p. 268.
19. Robertson, *McAllister Letters*, p. 438.
20. Miers, *Robert E. Lee: A Life-in-Brief*, p. 182.
21. Johnston, *Virginia Railroads*, p. 220.
22. *Ibid.*, p. 221.
23. Freeman, *Lee's Lieutenants*, III, 615.
24. Fuller, *Generalship of Grant*, p. 305.
25. Porter, *Campaigning with Grant*, pp. 300–01.
26. Sandburg, *Lincoln: The War Years*, III, 296–99.

CHAPTER 14. LINCOLN IN COMMAND

1. Sandburg, *Lincoln: The War Years*, III, 563–65.
2. Basler, *Collected Works*, VIII, 101.
3. *Ibid.*, pp. 136 *et seq.*
4. Dana, *Recollections of the Civil War*, p. 174.
5. *Ibid.*, p. 176.
6. Nicolay and Hay, *Lincoln*, X, 85–86.

CHAPTER 15. WITH MALICE TOWARD NONE

1. Miers, *Lee*, p. 181.
2. Basler, *Collected Works*, VIII, 356.
3. Angle and Miers, *Tragic Years*, II, 1010–11.
4. Letter to Isaac N. Arnold, November 28, 1877, *Ms*, Chicago Historical Society.
5. Porter, *Campaigning with Grant*, p. 426.
6. Angle and Miers, *Tragic Years*, II, 1015.
7. Davis, *The Rise and Fall of the Confederate Government*, p. 668.
8. Johnson and Buel, *Battles and Leaders*, IV, 725.
9. Bartlett, *History of the Twelfth Regiment New Hampshire Volunteers*, pp. 272–73.
10. Johnson and Buel, *Battles and Leaders*, IV, 727–28.
11. Eisenschiml and Newman, *American Iliad*, II, 131.
12. Livermore, *Numbers and Losses in the Civil War* . . . , pp. 110 *et seq.*
13. Bruce, *Lincoln and the Tools of War*, pp. ix–x.
14. *Ibid.*, p. 289.

EPILOGUE

1. John James Toffey, *Ms.*, RUL.
2. Basler, *Walt Whitman's Memoranda* . . . , p. 12.
3. Introduction, paperback edition, Davis's *The Rise and Fall of the Confederate Government*, pp. 11–12.
4. Author's field notes.

5. Nichols, *Blueprints for Leviathan*, pp. 216 *et seq.*

6. Davis, *The Rise and Fall of the Confederate Government*, II, 160–61.

7. Freeman, *R. E. Lee*, IV, 317.

8. Miers, *Lee*, pp. 196, 198.

9. Garland, "Ulysses Grant—His Last Year," *McClure's Magazine*, XI, 93.

10. Introduction, *The Rise and Fall of the Confederate Government*, pp. 17–18.

Bibliography

Adams, George Worthington. *Doctors in Blue*. New York: Henry Schuman, 1952.

Agassiz, George R., ed. *Meade's Headquarters, 1863–1865: Letters of Theodore Lyman from the Wilderness to Appomattox*. Boston: The Atlantic Monthly Press, 1922.

Alexander, Thomas G. "A Conflict of Perceptions: Ulysses S. Grant and the Mormons," *Newsletter* (Carbondale, Ill.: U. S. Grant Association), 1971.

Angle, Paul M., ed. *The Lincoln Reader*. New Brunswick, N.J.: Rutgers University Press, 1947.

————. *See* Dana, Charles A., *below*.

————, and Earl Schenck Miers, eds. *The Living Lincoln*. New Brunswick, N.J.: Rutgers University Press, 1955.

———— and ————, eds. *Tragic Years, 1860–1865*. New York: Simon & Schuster, Inc. 1960. 2 vols.

Atlantic Monthly. See Welles, Gideon.

Badeau, Adam. *Military History of Ulysses S. Grant*. New York: D. Appleton and Company, 1885. 3 vols.

Baringer, William E. "Lincoln 1809–1860." *See* Miers, Earl Schenck, ed., *Lincoln, Day-by-Day*.

Barthell, Edward E., Jr. *See* Livermore, Thomas L.

Bartlett, A. W. *History of the Twelfth Regiment New Hampshire Volunteers*. Concord, N.H.: privately printed, 1897.

Basler, Roy P., ed. *The Collected Works of Abraham Lincoln*. New Brunswick, N.J.: Rutgers University Press, 1953. 9 vols.

——, ed. *Walt Whitman's Memoranda During the War* [*and*] *Death of Abraham Lincoln.* Bloomington, Ind.: Indiana University Press, 1962.

Bates, David H. *Lincoln in the Telegraph Office of the United States Military Corps during the Civil War.* New York: The Century Company, 1907.

——, *Lincoln Stories Told by Him in the War Department During the Civil War.* New York: Rudge, 1926.

Beatty, Jerome, Jr., ed. *The Saturday Review Gallery.* New York: Simon & Schuster, Inc., 1959.

Bestor, Arthur, *et al. Three Presidents and Their Books: The Reading of Jefferson, Lincoln and Franklin D. Roosevelt.* Urbana, Ill.: University of Illinois Press, 1955.

Boatner, Mark Mayo, III. *The Civil War Dictionary.* New York: David McKay Company, 1959.

Brooks, Noah. *Washington, D.C., in Lincoln's Time.* Edited with an Introduction and New Preface by Herbert Mitgang. New York: Collier Books, 1962.

Bruce, Robert V. *Lincoln and the Tools of War.* Indianapolis: The Bobbs-Merrill Company, Inc., 1956.

Catton, Bruce. *Grant Moves South.* Boston: Little, Brown & Company, 1960.

——. *This Hallowed Ground: The Story of the Union Side of the Civil War.* Garden City, N.Y.: Doubleday & Company, Inc., 1956.

——. *See* Eisenschiml, Otto, and Ralph G. Newman.

Century Magazine. See Grover, Leonard.

Chicago Historical Society, General William Tecumseh Sherman to Isaac N. Arnold, November 28, 1877, MS.

Christian Advocate. See Wing, Henry E.

Churchill, Winston. *The American Civil War.* New York: Dodd, Mead & Company, Inc., 1961.

Cooke, John Esten. *Wearing of the Gray.* Edited and annotated by Philip Van Doren Stern. Bloomington, Ind.: Indiana University Press, 1959.

Dana, Charles A. *Recollections of the Civil War.* Edited by Paul M. Angle. New York: Collier Books, 1963 (Original edition, New York: D. Appleton and Company, 1898.)

Davis, Burke. *Jeb Stuart, The Last Cavalier.* New York: Rinehart & Company, Inc., 1957.

——. *See* McClellan, Henry B.

Davis, Jefferson. *The Rise and Fall of the Confederate Government.*

New York: D. Appleton and Company, 1910. 2 vols. (Paperback edition, New York: Collier Books, 1961.)

DeLeon, Thomas Cooper. *Four Years in Rebel Capitals*. Edited by E. B. Long. New York: Collier Books, 1962.

Dictionary of American Biography.

Donald, David, ed. *Why the North Won the Civil War*. Baton Rouge, La.: Louisiana State University Press, 1960.

Dowdey, Clifford. *Lee's Last Campaign: The Story of Lee and His Men, 1864*. Boston: Little, Brown & Company, 1960.

———, and Louis H. Manarin, eds. *The Wartime Papers of R. E. Lee*. Boston: Virginia Civil War Commission and Little, Brown & Company, 1961.

Dyer, Frederick H. *A Compendium of the War of the Rebellion*. Reissue, New York: Thomas Yoseloff, Inc., 1959. 3 vols.

Early, Jubal A. *Autobiographical Sketch and Narrative of the War Between the States*. Reissue, edited by Frank E. Vandiver. Bloomington, Ind.: Indiana University Press, 1960.

Eisenschiml, Otto, and Ralph G. Newman. *The Civil War: The American Iliad as Told by Those Who Lived It*. Introduction by Bruce Catton. New York: Grosset & Dunlap, 1956. 2 vols.

Freeman, Douglas Southall, ed. *Lee's Dispatches, Unpublished Letters of Robert E. Lee to Jefferson Davis*. New York: G. P. Putnam's Sons, 1957.

——— *Lee's Lieutenants: A Study in Command*. New York: Charles Scribner's Sons, 1942–44. 3 vols.

———., *R. E. Lee*. New York: Charles Scribner's Sons, 1951. 4 vols.

Fuller, J. F. C. *The Conduct of War, 1789–1961*. New Brunswick, N.J.: Rutgers University Press, 1961.

———. *The Generalship of Ulysses S. Grant*. Reissue, Bloomington, Ind.: Indiana University Press, 1958.

———., *Grant and Lee: A Study in Personality and Generalship*. Reissue, Bloomington, Ind.: Indiana University Press, 1957.

Garland, Hamlin. "Ulysses Grant—His Last Year," *McClure's Magazine*, XI.

Govan, Gilbert E., and James W. Livingood, eds. *The Haskell Memoirs*. New York: G. P. Putnam's Sons, 1960.

Grant, U. S., Association (Carbondale, Ill.). See Grant, Frederick D., Alexander, Thomas G.

Grant, Frederick D., "Extracts from an Address . . . ," *Proceedings of the Society of the Army of Tennessee* (Cincinnati), 1913; *Illinois*

Historical Journal (Springfield), 1914; *Newsletter* (Carbondale, Ill.: U.S. Grant Association), 1970.

Grant, Ulysses S. *Personal Memoirs of U. S. Grant.* Cleveland: World Publishing Company, 1952. Edited and annotated by E. B. Long. (Original edition, New York: Charles L. Webster & Company, 1885–86. 2 vols.)

Grover, Leonard. "Lincoln's Interest in the Theater," *Century Magazine*, LXXVII, April, 1909.

Haskell, John Cheeves. *See* Govan, Gilbert E., and James W. Livingood.

Henderson, G. F. R. *See* Luvass, Jay.

Hesseltine, William B. *Lincoln and the War Governors.* New York: Alfred A. Knopf, Inc., 1948.

Humphreys, Andrew A. *The Virginia Campaign of '64 and '65.* New York: Charles Scribner's Sons, 1894.

Hyman, Harold M. *See* Thomas, Benjamin P.

Johnson, Robert U., and Clarence C. Buel, eds. *Battles and Leaders of the Civil War.* New York: The Century Company, 1884–88. 4 vols.

Johnston, Angus James, II. *Virginia Railroads in the Civil War.* Chapel Hill, N.C.: The Virginia Historical Society and the University of North Carolina Press, 1961.

Jones, John B. *A Rebel War Clerk's Diary.* Edited by Earl Schenck Miers. New York: Sagamore Press, Inc., 1958.

Lee, Robert E. *See* Dowdey, Clifford, and Louis H. Manarin.

Lee, Robert E., Jr. *My Father, General Lee.* Garden City, N.Y.: Doubleday & Company, Inc., 1960.

Leech, Margaret. *Reveille in Washington, 1860–1865.* New York: Harper and Brothers, 1941.

Lewis, Lloyd. *Captain Sam Grant.* Boston: Little, Brown & Company, 1950.

Lincoln, Abraham. *See* Basler, Roy P.

Lincoln Day-by-Day. See Miers, Earl Schenck.

Livermore, Thomas L. *Numbers and Losses in the Civil War in America: 1861–65.* Reissue, edited by Edward E. Barthell, Jr. Bloomington, Ind.: Indiana University Press, 1957.

Long, E. B. *See* DeLeon, Thomas Cooper; Grant, Ulysses S.; Rhodes, James Ford.

Longstreet, James B. *From Manassas to Appomattox.* Reissue, edited and annotated by James I. Robertson, Jr. Bloomington, Ind.: Indiana University Press, 1960.

Luvass, Jay, ed. *The Civil War: A Soldier's View* by Colonel G. F. R. Henderson. Chicago: University of Chicago Press, 1958.

Lyman, Theodore. *See* Agassiz, George R.

McAllister, Robert. *See* Robertson, James I., Jr.

Macartney, Edward Clarence. *Grant and His Generals.* New York: Robert M. McBride & Company, 1953.

McClellan, Henry B. *I Rode with Jeb Stuart.* Reissue, edited by Burke Davis. Bloomington, Ind.: Indiana University Press, 1958.

————. article, Southern Historical Society Papers, VII.

McClure, Alexander Kelly. *Lincoln and Men of War Times.* Edited by J. Stuart Torrey, with an Introduction by Earl Schenck Miers. Reissue, Philadelphia: Rolley & Reynolds, Inc., 1962.

McClure's Magazine. See Garland, Hamlin.

McPherson, Edward. *The Political History of the United States . . . during the Great Rebellion.* Washington, D.C., 1865.

Marbaker, Thomas D. *History of the Eleventh New Jersey Volunteers.* Trenton, 1898.

Mearns, David C., "Lincoln," *Three Presidents and Their Books: The Reading of Jefferson, Lincoln, and Franklin D. Roosevelt,* Arthur Bestor, ed. Urbana, Ill.: University of Illinois Press, 1955.

Miers, Earl Schenck. *The General Who Marched to Hell: William Tecumseh Sherman.* New York: Alfred A. Knopf, Inc., 1951.

————. *The Great Rebellion.* New York: World Publishing Company, 1958.

————, ed. *Lincoln Day-by-Day.* Washington, D.C.: Lincoln Sesquicentennial Commission, 1960. Vols. 1 and 2: *Lincoln 1809–1860,* compiled by William E. Baringer; vol. 3: *1861–1865,* compiled by C. Percy Powell.

————, ed. *Ride to War. See* Pyne, Henry R.

————. *Robert E. Lee: A Life-in-Brief.* New York: Alfred A. Knopf, Inc., 1956.

————. "When in Doubt, Fight." *See* Beatty, Jerome, Jr.

————. *See* Angle, Paul M.; Jones, John B.; McClure, Alexander Kelly.

Mitgang, Herbert. *See* Brooks, Noah.

Moore, Frank A., ed. *The Rebellion Record: A Diary of American Events.* New York: D. Van Nostrand Company, Inc., 1864–68, 11 vols.

Mordell, Albert, ed. *Selected Essays by Gideon Welles.* New York: Twayne Publishers, 1960.

Morison, Samuel Eliot. *The Oxford History of the American People.* New York: Oxford University Press, 1965.

Murphy, D. F. *Proceedings of the National Union Convention.* New York: Baker and Godwin, 1864.

Nevins, Allan. *The War For the Union.* New York: Charles Scribner's Sons, 1959. 6 vols.

————. *See* Strong, George Templeton.

Newman, Ralph G. *See* Eisenschiml, Otto.

Nichols, Roy F. *Blueprints for Leviathan: American Style.* New York: Atheneum Publishers, 1963.

Nicolay, Helen. *Lincoln's Secretary: A Biography of John G. Nicolay.* New York: Longmans, Green & Company, 1949.

Nicolay, John G., and John Hay. *Abraham Lincoln: A History.* New York: The Century Company, 1890. 10 vols.

Official Records. See War of the Rebellion.

Porter, Horace M. *Campaigning with Grant.* New York: The Century Company, 1897.

Powell, C. Percy, "1861–1865." *See* Miers, Earl Schenck, ed., *Lincoln Day-by-Day.*

Pyne, Henry R. *History of the First New Jersey Cavalry.* Trenton: J. A. Beecher, 1871. Reissued as *Ride to War,* edited and annotated by Earl Schenck Miers. New Brunswick, N.J.: Rutgers University Press, 1961.

Rebellion Record. See Moore, Frank A.

Rembert, Patrick W. *Jefferson Davis and His Cabinet.* Baton Rouge, La.: Louisiana State University Press, 1944.

Rhodes, James Ford. *History of the Civil War.* Reissue, edited by E. B. Long. New York: Frederick Ungar Publishing Company, 1961.

Richmond Examiner. Account of the death of Jeb Stuart, Southern Historical Society Papers, VII.

Robertson, James I., Jr. *The Civil War Letters of General Robert McAllister.* New Brunswick, N.J.: The New Jersey Civil War Centennial Commission and Rutgers University Press, 1965. Abstracted from the original manuscripts in the Rutgers University Library.

————. *See* Taylor, Walter H.; Longstreet, James.

Roebling, Washington A. Unpublished papers in the Rutgers University Library.

Sandburg, Carl. *Abraham Lincoln: The War Years.* New York: Harcourt, Brace and Company, 1939. 4 vols.

Schenck, Martin. *Up Came Hill: The Story of the Light Division and Its Leaders.* Harrisburg, Pa.: The Stackpole Company, 1958.

Sheridan, Philip H. *Personal Memoirs.* New York: D. Appleton and Company, 1904. 2 vols.

Society of the Army of Tennessee. *See* Grant, Frederick D.

Sorrel, G. Moxley. *Recollections of a Confederate Staff Officer.* Edited by Bell Irvin Wiley. Jackson, Tenn.: McCowat-Mercer Press, Inc., 1958.

Southern Historical Society Papers. *See* McClellan, H. B.; *Richmond Examiner.*

Starr, Louis M. *Bohemian Brigade: Civil War Newsmen in Action.* New York: Alfred A. Knopf, Inc., 1954.

Steere, Edward. *The Wilderness Campaign.* Harrisburg, Pa.: The Stackpole Company, 1960.

Stern, Philip Van Doren. *See* Cooke, John Esten.

Strode, Hudson. *Jefferson Davis, Confederate President.* New York: Harcourt, Brace and Company, 1959.

Strong, George Templeton, *Diary, 1835–1875.* Edited by Allan Nevins and Milton H. Thomas. New York: The Macmillan Company, 1952. 4 vols.

Swinton, William. *Campaigns of the Army of the Potomac.* New York: Charles B. Richardson, 1866.

Tarbell, Ida M. *All in the Day's Work.* New York: The Macmillan Company, 1939.

Taylor, Walter H. *Four Years with General Lee.* Edited by James I. Robertson, Jr. Reissue, Bloomington, Ind.: Indiana University Press, 1962.

Thomas, Benjamin P. *Abraham Lincoln.* New York: Alfred A. Knopf, Inc., 1952.

——— and Harold M. Hyman. *Stanton: The Life and Times of Lincoln's Secretary of War.* New York: Alfred A. Knopf, Inc., 1962.

Thomas, Milton H. *See* Strong, George Templeton.

Toffey, John James. Unpublished papers in the Rutgers University Library.

Tucker, Glenn. *Hancock the Superb.* Indianapolis: The Bobbs-Merrill Company, 1960.

Vandiver, Frank E. *Jubal's Raid: General Early's Famous Attack on Washington in 1864.* New York: McGraw-Hill Book Company, Inc., 1960.

———. *See* Early, Jubal A.

War of the Rebellion: . . . Official Records of the Union and Confederate Armies. Washington, D.C., 1880–1901. 128 vols.

Welles, Gideon. *Diary.* New York: Houghton Mifflin Company, 1911. 3 vols.

———. "Lincoln's Triumph in 1864," *Atlantic Monthly,* March, 1878. Vol. 41.

———. *See* Mordell, Albert.

Werstein, Irving. *Abraham Lincoln versus Jefferson Davis*. New York: Thomas Y. Crowell Company, 1959.

Whitman, Walt. *See* Basler, Roy P.

Wiley, Bell Irvin. *See* Sorrel, G. Moxley.

Williams, T. Harry. *Lincoln and His Generals*. New York: Alfred A. Knopf, Inc., 1952.

——. "The Military Leadership of the North and South." *See* David Donald, ed., *Why the North Won the Civil War*.

Wilson, James H. *Under the Old Flag*. New York: D. Appleton and Company, 1912. 2 vols.

Wing, Henry E. "Stories of a War Correspondent," *Christian Advocate*, Vols. 88–90.

——. *When Lincoln Kissed Me: A Story of the Wilderness Campaign*. New York: Eaton & Movins, 1913.

Index